Marygrove
EX LIBRIS

267.1
Sw 2

267.11
Su2t

THEOLOGY OF THE APOSTOLATE

Mgr. LEON JOSEPH SUENENS
AUXILIARY BISHOP OF MALINES

THEOLOGY OF THE APOSTOLATE

OF THE
LEGION OF MARY

WITH LETTER OF PAPAL APPROBATION

THE NEWMAN PRESS
WESTMINSTER, MARYLAND

BY THE SAME AUTHOR

THEOLOGY OF THE APOSTOLATE OF THE LEGION OF MARY
French 4th edition, Descles de Brouwer, Bruges;
Dutch: Sheed and Ward, Antwerp;
Italian: Coletti, Rome;
Spanish: Desclee, Bilbao;
German: Rohr, Fribourg and Heiler, Vienna;
Chinese: Hma Ming Press, Hongkong;
In preparation, Japanese, Korean, Slovac, Portuguese editions.

A HEROINE OF APOSTOLATE. Edel-Mary Quinn: 1907-1944
(Concilium Legionis, Dublin).

QUE FAUT IL PENSER DU REARMEMENT MORAL?
(Edition Universitaire, Paris).
English translation in preparation.

First Published in U.S.A. by
The Newman Press,
Westminster, Maryland

Printed in the Republic of Ireland
by the Kerryman Ltd., Russell Street, Tralee

Dal Vaticano, December 6, 1952.

DI SUA SANTITA

N. 288814.

My Lord Bishop,
I am glad to inform your Excellency of the Sovereign Pontiff's gratitude for the presentation copy of your fine book 'Theology of the Apostolate of the Legion of Mary.'

This spiritual commentary on the Legionary Promise brings out very clearly the value of the apostolic and Marian pledge which has already strengthened in their struggle in Christ's service so many members of the Legion, scattered throughout the world, and those especially who, at the present time, are suffering persecution for their faith.

Therefore, the Holy Father heartily congratulates you on your work. It will, doubtless, provide many Catholics with a clearer insight into an apostolate which, over and above the necessary duties of the temporal order, of set purpose intends to serve the sacred cause of the Kingdom of God. Also, in meditating on your substantial pages, they will come to a better understanding of the extent to which apostolic action must draw its inspiration from her who gave Jesus Christ to the world and still remains in His sight the pattern of Christian holiness and the channel of all graces.

This reminder of these principles which in no way prejudice the legitimate diversity of apostolic methods, has already encountered a wide welcome, far beyond Legion of Mary circles: this is indeed matter for rejoicing. His Holiness gladly wishes that your book may continue its beneficent work and, as a pledge of the graces that He implores for you and your labours, with all His heart bestows on you the Apostolic Blessing.

I am glad to pass on to you this august message and ask you to accept, my Lord, the assurance of my own high regard.

His Excellency
Mgr. Leon Joseph Suenens, *Auxiliary Bishop of Malines.*
(Signed) J. B. Montini,
Prosecr.

Malines,
10th January, 1951.

Excellency,
When we entrusted you with the direction of the Legion of Mary in our diocese you desired to find out about the organisation and spiritual value of this apostolic movement of which so many wonderful things are recounted. You went, therefore, to the fountain head whence it sprang with such surprising strength, and on different occasions journeyed to Dublin to obtain an authentic picture of the spirit whence it drew its great driving power. For the Legion of Mary was born in the mystic climate of Catholic Ireland; there is no cause for astonishment that in this soil, so steeped in faith, it burgeoned into a great tree whose branches spread across the world.

On the other hand you were able to see, as the work took root here in Belgium, what wonderful results it produced in souls: conversions, return of the lapsed, frequentation of the sacraments, support and development of established works. Such results soon enabled you to appreciate the real apostolic value of the Legion of Mary. Its rapid growth, and the profound influence it exerts upon souls, show very clearly that it is a capital means of bringing grace into play; it can be clearly felt that 'the finger of God is here.'

Can we be surprised at this when we see the place held by the Blessed Virgin Mary in this movement which not only fights under her blessed name, but is conscious also of fulfilling her own especial work of mediation. In our times the whole life of the Church bears the mark of the world-wide filial devotion of all the faithful to the Mother of God and, conversely of the profound, mysterious action which the Mediatrix of all Graces is pleased to exert in the world. By the definition of the dogma of the Assumption, at which we had the signal honour of being present, the Church set her indefectible seal on the Marian age in which we are fortunate enough to live.

Taking all these facts into consideration and seeking some explanation of them you wished to elucidate the principles which are behind this remarkable apostolic movement, and in this way explain its extraordinary success; on this basis you have endeavoured to work out a Theology of the Apostolate of service to all. Of its nature, therefore, your book is addressed as much to the educated layman as to the priest. We invite them to meditate on these substantial pages and to think out under your direction the source of all true apostolic action.

You demonstrate how the apostolate is bound up with the Holy Ghost and Our Lady; it is striking to see how this combination, nowadays as formerly, presides over the bringing forth of Christ. Et incarnatus est de Spiritu Sancto ex Maria Virgine: therein lies the key to your book and also its particular efficacy. From that first principle your whole work is derived and inevitably, almost, the corollaries for action emerge clearly from it. The apostolate that you have in mind is primarily the direct, evangelical, religious apostolate founded, as you point out, on the Acts of the Apostles.

You call on Christians to strengthen their faith and to communicate it to others with courage and confidence. Too many of them, in order to remain inactive, shelter behind flimsy excuses; you show clearly how vain such excuses are. For the Church, as for the world, grave times are upon us; no one has the right to remain unconcerned about the salvation of his fellows.

May your appeal be heard. May it raise up for the clergy innumerable fellow-workers among all ranks of the faithful. Now, more than ever, we need the efficient help of the laity in building and extending the Kingdom of God.

The lofty theological considerations with which the Legionary Promise has inspired you will prove, no doubt, an excellent subject for meditation for members of the Legion of Mary and a powerful stimulant to ever greater thoroughness in their apostolic work.

May the most Blessed Virgin, whom you desired to serve in writing these pages so filled with doctrine and devotion, deign to bestow upon them her maternal blessing and to open hearts and minds to their message.

✠ *J. E. Cardinal van Roey,*
Archbishop of Malines.

CONTENTS

CHAPTER		Page
	FOREWORD	xi
I.	THE HOLY GHOST	1
	1. The Nature of the Love of God	1
	2. The Particular Function of the Holy Spirit within the Blessed Trinity	3
	3. The Function of the Holy Spirit in the Church	4
	4. Deference to the Action of God	9
II.	OUR LADY	13
	1. The Partnership of the Holy Ghost with Our Blessed Lady	13
	2. The Faithfulness of the Alliance	15
	3. The Holy Ghost forming Christ in us	18
	4. Our Lady forming Christ in us	23
III.	MARIAN MEDIATION	27
	1. The Mediation of Mary ascending towards God	27
	2. Mediation of Mary descending towards Men	37
IV.	UNION WITH MARY	41
	1. The Way of Childhood: 'In Sinu Matris'	41
	2. Union with Mary, the Way to God	42
	3. Union with Mary, the Way to Men's Hearts	49
V.	APOSTOLIC COURAGE	57
	1. Courage, a Necessary Virtue	58
	2. Courage, a Marian Virtue	61
	3. Courage in the Face of the Impossible	63
	4. Courage and latent Heroism	67

VI.	HUMILITY AND APOSTOLIC STRENGTH	70
	1. The Humility of Our Lady	70
	2. Legionary Humility	72
	3. Daring, a Virtue of the Humble	75
	4. Audacity and the Conversion of the Masses	78
VII.	PURITY AND SPIRITUAL GROWTH	82
	1. Apostolic Purity	82
	2. Our Lady's Purity	83
	3. Our Growth in Christ	88
	4. Awaiting Christ	92
VIII.	PRAYER AND ACTION	96
	1. Prayer	96
	2. Action	106
IX.	MARIAN MEDIATIONS	118
	1. The early Dawn of Mediation: the Visitation	118
	2. The Sunrise of Mediation: Pentecost	122
	3. The broad Daylight of Mediation at the present Day	125
X.	MARY, THE CHURCH, AND THE WORLD	132
	1. Mary and the Church in General	132
	2. Mary and the Church in the World today	135
XI.	THE SIGN OF THE CROSS	140
	1. Suffering and the Apostolate	140
	2. The Compassion of Mary	145
	3. The Sign of the Cross	148
	4. Profession of Faith in the Trinity	148
	NOTES	153

FOREWORD

ON SEPTEMBER 7, 1921, at first Vespers of the Nativity of our Lady, in silence and simplicity, the Legion of Mary was born. Fifteen people had arranged to meet at Myra House to find together ways of serving the Lord. Spontaneously they knelt before a statue of Mary Mediatrix and said the Rosary to ask her inspiration and guidance. They did not know what apostolic tasks were to be entrusted to them and still less how to carry them out. With unbounded confidence each offered to his Queen the little that he possessed: his fears, his poverty and an absolute good will. Our Lady might do with them whatever she wished for the salvation of the world.

The most blessed Virgin accepted their gift, as Jesus once accepted the five loaves and two fishes that a young man brought to him to feed a multitude. And in her hands the marvel of multiplication was renewed.

That original nucleus has become legion, and in a quarter of a century by its very dynamism has spread throughout five continents. Everywhere, in every latitude, men and women have repeated that first gesture; they have knelt to pray together, and then have offered themselves to Mary that her motherhood of grace might be put into action among men.

Today, an immense army of our Lady acknowledges her as its head. Its rallying cry is that which the Church attributes to the angels on the dawn of the Assumption:

'Who is she that cometh forth as the morning rising, fair as the moon, bright as the sun, terrible as an army set in array?'

If success is to follow, there must be a spiritual alliance between the head and his troops. We know what his oath of allegiance, consecrating him to loyal service, meant to the knight of the middle ages. The Legionary of Mary, too, knows the joy and emotion of pledging his word. The Promise that he makes among his brethren, the Vexillum in hand, is a contract linking him to his Mother and consecrating to her service whatever he is or he possesses. It is an alliance which places him wholly at her disposal 'for better, for worse,' for every task that she confides to him for the salvation of mankind and which gives him, under her device and seal, a desire for union tending to unity of the highest degree.

The words of this Promise are pregnant with meaning and rich in consequences. Some of its phrases stand out clearcut, struck like a medal. Such words should not merely touch the surface of the soul but be engraved on memory and heart.

That is why we have thought it worthwhile to write these pages. They are designed to give the Legionary a fuller understanding of his pledge, to enable him to penetrate deeply, to scrutinize and measure carefully the full meaning of this formula by which he is bound. We know few prayers in contemporary Christian literature which are of such density and arouse such spiritual echoes.

To grasp its vital import the adventure that it proffers must be accepted; only those who are unafraid to live the love of God which animates this pledge will discover its whole meaning. For several, no doubt, these words, like so many others, will remain but words, heard already and so classified; but he who accepts the contract of alliance, and lives it down the years, will understand it from within.

The Legionary, then, must prove the Promise by living it and thus penetrate it ever more deeply. He should read it and re-read it continually.

To the new member, preparing for his consecration, we offer these pages as an introduction and a guide. To the veteran, we present them as an invitation to steep himself again at the source during retreat or when making a renewal of the Promise. Both of them we entreat not to be content with one rapid reading, but to pray these pages. That is, to open them with an invocation of the Holy Ghost who alone can help us to 'contemplate the depths of God,' and to savour them, and to close them with another prayer, asking the Holy Ghost for the generous docility, the whole-hearted welcome of it that will enable us to live this apostolic gift. For at no moment is it our concern alone; an offering to the Holy Ghost in and through Mary is made so that the world may be saved and the Acts of the Apostles continue. 'I come to bring fire on earth,' our Lord told us, 'and will that it should continue.'

This fire is the Holy Ghost to whom the Legionary offers his soul as a torch so that its flame may set other souls ablaze till the whole world is alight.

*
* *

We hope that these pages will prove more than a mere commentary on the Promise. We mean them to be an introduction to Legionary spirituality itself. In addition they are addressed, therefore, to the non-Legionary reader in search of information about the spirit of this movement which has taken so great a place in the Church that it can no longer be ignored; more especially as its growth becomes, daily, more marked.

For the Legion of Mary, after thirty years of life and experience, seems only at its beginnings. Born in Ireland, in 1921, it crossed those frontiers only in 1928, to be established in dioceses in England and then in India and America. It conquered Asia, Australia and Africa, before reaching European countries. At the present time the prayers of the Legion are said in nigh on seventy languages and its active and auxiliary members amount to millions. Some seven hundred bishops have made it welcome in their dioceses and their testimony commands attention. The Internuncio to China, Mgr. Riberi, invited the bishops of China to establish it everywhere, as a kind of spiritual underground movement in the Church, and described it as the 'miracle of the modern world.'

In view of these facts a question arises, *Quae est ista?* What is this movement and what is the key to its success? That is the question that we hope to answer in describing the fundamental characteristics of the Legion of Mary and in analysing its spirituality.

That last word may suggest that the Legion lays claim to some unspecified exclusive or special teaching of its own. In fact, as we hope to show, the Legion implies living a normal Catholicism, normal, it should be emphasized, not average.

Nowadays we are apt to think of the normal Catholic as one who practises his religion on his own account without worrying himself about the salvation of others. This is a caricature of the faithful Catholic and indeed of Catholicism. The average Catholic is not the *normal* Catholic. The notion of a 'good Catholic' or a 'practising Catholic' requires close examination and should be subjected to considerable revision. One cannot be a Catholic if one falls short of a certain minimum of apostolic activity, and this indispensable minimum, which will be fully taken into account at the last judgment, is not achieved by the mass of 'practising' Catholics. Therein lies the tragedy and the fundamental misunderstanding.

All that is said here about the duty of the lay apostolate—it will be mentioned again—which is an essential feature of the Legion, could be said equally well of its devotion to our Lady. The Legion loves Mary as the Church does, no more no less, that is to say, exceedingly.

The Legion does not wish to pray, as it were, in a side chapel but in the central nave; it was not the Legion which decreed that Mary is at the very heart of Christianity, and that Christians, by a process analogous to that which gave Jesus Christ to the world, are born of 'the Holy Ghost and of Mary.'

The Legion intends to practise normal devotion to our Lady, that is, Christian devotion. If this ambition leads far, if the gift of self follows in the wake of this inspiration, it is because Christ himself desires to continue loving his Mother in us, and urges us to extend our filial love to the measure of his own.

For it should not be forgotten that the Son of God chose to be the son of Mary. He loves His Mother—chosen by Him from among thousands upon thousands—with an incomparable love, far superior to that which He bears towards all the angels and saints together. He bestowed on her privileges which He did not give to the Seraphim, He associated her as no other with His work of redemption, and it is He who, through His Spirit, presides over the ever-increasing glorification of Mary in the Church of our times.

If 'I live now not I: but Christ liveth in me' (*Gal.* 11, 20), is it not natural that if I love Mary it is not I, but Christ in me, loving her? Because He is the crown of human nature, our love for her is but one with His and He it is who, in us, exercises and expresses it in ways ever new. St. Paul could say 'I fill up those things that are wanting of the sufferings of Christ in my flesh' (*Col.* 1, 24). In Christ Himself nothing was wanting in His Passion, but there was something lacking in Paul, a member of the whole Christ. Analogously, I can complete in myself what is lacking in the filial piety of Christ towards His Mother.

The Legion desires simply to love Mary with the Heart of Christ, as it endeavours to love Christ with the heart of Mary. Since this is God's will and design, it accepts it with faith and with no timidity or reserve.

Doctrinally it claims no greater originality than that. It is fidelity—and where necessary a return—to authentic tradition. This is its ideal and aim. If, then, we use the term Legionary spirituality it is solely to mark those characteristics set in strong relief against the common heritage of the Church's children. If sometimes the Legion causes astonishment by its requirements it is due to no seeking after the unusual but is the consequence of its concern to live a full and vigorous Christianity.

Why must many so-called 'practising' Catholics live in a way falling very short of their baptism? How our scale of values would be transformed if, instead of judging Christianity by that distorted standard, we could only see it in the light of Christ. What a revolution would result if, with no compromise, we would only follow to the letter the teachings of the Master.

It may be said that it is the Legion's ambition to answer by stern fact the question: 'What would happen now in the twentieth century, if anyone dared to take literally Christ's words about faith that moves mountains?' The history of the Legion—as beautiful as the Golden Legend—provides the answer: 'The blind see, the lame walk, the lepers are cleansed, the deaf hear, the dead rise again, the poor have the Gospel preached to them.' (*Matt.* 11, 5). ([1])

The principles behind this evangelistic work hold good for all apostolic action worthy of the name, whether it is general or specialized Catholic Action. The apostolate, an extension of the Incarnation itself, is effected always and everywhere *de Spiritu Sancto ex Maria Virgine*. Points of view and methods of execution may vary legitimately, but its inspiration, its essential spirit, is common to all forms.

Like all supernatural realities, the Christian apostolate has two aspects and envisages two worlds. There is the human side, turned towards the terrestrial world, where the apostle comes to grips with an infinite variety of men, situations, classes, and ages. Here divine teaching will have to be adapted and thus knowledge is required of the conditions under which the spiritual preparation of the ground can be carried out. But there is also the heavenly side of apostolic labour, whose laws are as unchangeable and universal as the Church itself. This is the aspect which is emphasized in these pages. All genuine apostolate must be Marian lest it be but a stunted growth. The Legion of Mary is a living incarnation of these principles but it makes no claim to a monopoly of them. Freely it fraternizes with all other, and equally necessary, forms of organization which must each be steeped in the same life-giving springs.

May the teaching set forth in these pages be of help to all who work side by side in the vineyard of the Lord, and may it sustain their enthusiasm.

THE PROMISE OF THE LEGION

*Most Holy Spirit, I, (Name of the Candidate),
Desiring to be enrolled this day as a Legionary of Mary,
Yet knowing that of myself I cannot render worthy service,
Do ask of Thee to come upon me and fill me with Thyself,
So that my poor acts may be sustained by Thy power, and become an instrument of Thy mighty purposes.
But I know that Thou, who hast come to regenerate the world in Jesus Christ,
Hast not willed to do so except through Mary;
That without her we cannot know or love Thee;
That it is by her, and to whom she pleases, when she pleases, and in the quantity and manner she pleases,
That all Thy gifts and virtues and graces are administered;
And I realise that the secret of a perfect Legionary service
Consists in a complete union with her who is so completely united to Thee.
So, taking in my hand the Legionary Standard, which seeks to set before our eyes these things,
I stand before Thee as her soldier and her child,
And I so declare my entire dependence on her.
She is the mother of my soul.
Her heart and mine are one;
And from that single heart she speaks again those words of old:
'Behold the handmaid of the Lord';
And once again Thou comest by her to do great things.
Let Thy power overshadow me, and come into my soul with fire and love.
And make it one with Mary's love and Mary's will to save the world;
So that I may be pure in her who was made Immaculate by Thee;*

So that Christ my Lord may likewise grow in me through Thee;
So that I with her, His Mother, may bring Him to the world and to the souls who need Him;
So that they and I, the battle won, may reign with her for ever in the glory of the Blessed Trinity.
Confident that Thou wilt so receive me—and use me—and turn my weakness into strength this day,
I take my place in the ranks of the Legion, and I venture to promise a faithful service.
I will submit fully to its discipline,
Which binds me to my comrades,
And shapes us to an army,
And keeps our line as on we march with Mary,
To work Thy will, to operate Thy miracles of grace,
Which will renew the face of the earth,
And establish Thy reign, Most Holy Spirit, over all.
In the name of the Father and of the Son and of the Holy Ghost, Amen.

CHAPTER I.

THE HOLY GHOST

MOST HOLY SPIRIT . . .
DESIRING TO BE ENROLLED AS A LEGIONARY OF MARY, YET KNOWING THAT OF MYSELF I CANNOT RENDER WORTHY SERVICE, DO ASK OF THEE TO COME UPON ME AND FILL ME WITH THYSELF, SO THAT MY POOR ACTS MAY BE SUSTAINED BY THY POWER, AND BECOME AN INSTRUMENT OF THY MIGHTY PURPOSES.

1. *The Nature of the Love of God.*

MOST HOLY SPIRIT. . . . It is by direct appeal to the Spirit of God that the promise begins. To Him the whole pledge is taken.

He is the beginning as He is the end. He is the Love whence sprang the world, just as He is Love who will one day be All in All. That is why the soul of the Legionary is turned towards Him in making this dedicatory gesture which will affect His whole life.

The Legionary knows that his offering is only an answer, his love an acknowledgment, an adherence to another Love. He knows that he is giving himself up to One who first gave Himself. God loved us first, and it is that which governs our spiritual impulsion towards Him. In this alliance the initiative is not ours. Earth does not climb heavenwards, heaven comes down to earth, freely, generously and, seeing human ingratitude, one might dare to say, foolishly. For God had nothing to gain from the exchange. He could neither augment nor enrich Himself for He is the ultimate completeness. He was and is Love, sufficient to itself yet ever lavishing itself, unfathomably generous, inimitably benevolent.

It is astonishing not that God is, but that we are: we, who can give nothing to Him, add nothing to His magnificence, offer Him nothing to intensify His bliss, His personal joy. God shares with no one the glory of loving us freely, with unequalled magnanimity.

When a man lays down his life for another he is necessarily enriched by his sacrifice, necessarily ennobled by the very act which humbles and effaces him. Whether we will or no, a completely disinterested love is not within our reach; it is an attribute of God. And it is with this love, complete and all-embracing, that God loves us.

It is a comforting truth, for if the love of God springs solely from Himself, if there is no reason for love but love, then there is nothing that can cause the tenderness of God to waver; not our wretchedness, nor our cowardice, nor yet our falls in the mire. His love for us is not a return, for it came first. His love does not depend upon our own goodness, for it creates in us all that is lovable. His love itself provides the object for His love. This gives Him an extraordinary power, enabling Him to love us, if we may so put it, relentlessly.

Francis Thompson extolled such love in his immortal lines:

> Strange, piteous, futile thing
> Wherefore should any set thee love apart?
> Seeing none but I makes much of naught.   (*He said*)
> 'And human love needs human meriting:
> How hast thou merited—
> Of all man's clotted clay the dingiest clot!
> Alack, thou knowest not
> How little worthy of any love thou art!
> Whom wilt thou find to love ignoble thee,
> Save Me, save only Me?'
>   *The Hound of Heaven.* (²)

2. *The Particular Function of the Holy Spirit within the Blessed Trinity.*

All this we must bear in mind when we turn towards that primal love which we call the Holy Ghost, the Paraclete.

It was with this royal, creative love that God loved Mary —and us in her—when He came to her on that morning of the Annunciation.

Christianity might be defined as an exchange of two loves in the person of Jesus Christ: love descending from heaven to effect this sacred alliance—the Holy Spirit; love rising from earth to meet Him—Mary.

Doubtless this love which, in Mary, is raised up to meet the Holy Ghost, is a participation in divine love itself. More than any other creature, Mary received the fullness of heavenly grace. She loves God with that same love with which He loves her; and it was from the depth of the mysterious communication that God made to her of Himself, that she answered the call of divine love.

Yet it remains true that Mary's role is the authentic response of the creature sanctified for a divine vocation. Mary is the final culmination of the plan, developed through long ages by the God of the Old Testament, to make of Israel God's people, a bride 'blessed in truth and in holiness.' In Mary 'the earth brings forth her fruits' and 'salvation has rained from the skies.' *Terra dabit fructum suum et nubes pluant justum*: this vow, this promise with which the Old Testament is full, is effected in Mary.

At the meeting place of God and man, in Israel, God's chosen people, stands the Incarnation with all its consequences.

We dare, then, to consider closely Him who so fruitfully overshadowed Mary, and to explore the mysteries of the Spirit 'on whom the angels desire to look.' (*I Peter* 1, 12).

We know of course, that the works of God effected outside Himself are common to the Three Divine Persons: the love of

God which enfolds and penetrates us is a threefold and single gift, a threefold and single love. But though His role includes those of the other Persons, the Holy Ghost does not hide Himself under the anonymity of the Trinity. For though the works of God 'ad extra' (outside Himself) are common to all Three Persons of the Trinity, each Person has His own function, which is individual and in no sense interchangeable.[3] Certainly also, the Holy Spirit does not work alone at our sanctification, still less does He work to the exclusion of the other Persons. God the Father makes us holy, as does God the Son, but each in His own way: the First Person sanctifies us as a Father sending to us, with and through the Son, the Third Person, the Holy Ghost, Himself at once their supreme gift and the seal of their mutual love. Receiving the Holy Spirit we enter into the intimacy of kinship with the Godhead.

The Father, says St. Athanasius, is the spring, the Son is the torrent and we drink of the Spirit.[4] The Greek Fathers are fond of repeating this in all sorts of ways. The Holy Ghost, we might say, ushers us into the life of God. He is the fruit of the union between Father and Son; He is also the link between God and man, especially between God and Mary. It is as though He were the hand of the arm that God holds out to men. He it is in whom we possess the Son and the Father. Everything proceeds from the Father through the Son in the Holy Ghost. This axiom is the constant theme in Eastern Catholic literature. The universal Church in the development of the liturgical cycle centres her seasons—Advent, Lent and Pentecost—upon the Father, the Son and the Holy Ghost, respectively, making use of this Trinitarian dynamism to enable us to live in harmony with this divine spiritual rhythm.

3. *The Function of the Holy Spirit in the Church.*

It was towards the Holy Spirit that Christ Himself turned the souls of His apostles when He took leave of them: 'But I say unto you the truth: it is expedient to you that I go. For if I go not, the Paraclete will not come to you: but if I go I will send Him to you.' (*John* 16, 7).

The coming of the Holy Ghost was Christ's last promise, the pledge of His presence and even of His victory. When on the morning of Pentecost the Holy Spirit came down on the apostles gathered in the cenacle, a new era began for the world, the era of the Holy Ghost, the fullness of time.

For strictly speaking it is through Him that we have entered upon this latest phase of the world's history. Henceforward, if it may be so expressed, the centre of the stage belongs to Him. It was He who transformed Galilean fishermen, who came down upon the early Christians, flooding them with His *charismata*, who imbued the martyrs with His irresistible power, beginning with St. Stephen, *plenus fide et Spiritu Sancto*, filled with faith and the Holy Ghost.

The Acts of the Apostles, which open the history of the Church, are, in fact, nothing but the 'Gospel of the Holy Ghost.'

At his very first contact with the crowd at Pentecost, St. Peter applied to the Holy Ghost these words of Joel:

> 'But this is that which was spoken of by the prophet Joel: And it shall come to pass in the last days (saith the Lord) I will pour out of my Spirit upon all flesh: and your sons and your daughters shall prophesy: and your young men shall see visions: and your old men shall dream dreams. And upon my servants indeed, and upon my handmaids will I pour out in those days of my Spirit: and they shall prophesy . . . before the great and manifold day of the Lord come.' (*Acts* 2, 16-20; *Joel* 3, 1-5, in the Hebrew text).

While we wait for this Parousia, when the majesty of God shall be revealed to us, the Holy Ghost, is constantly at work. Every page of the Acts glows with His presence, far more vital, far more vigorous than the men whose histories are recorded and whose names we read. They speak of Him as of a personal presence, steadfast and beloved. Even though St. Luke does not mention Him by name he is present like a metallic thread running through every sacred page. He is the great apostolic designer, weaving in the hidden threads.

He, it was, who suggested the words to be spoken before the Sanhedrin, the proconsuls or the governors of Rome; just as He was the inspiration of the daily sermons:

> 'And my speech and my preaching was not in the persuasive words of human wisdom, but in shewing of the Spirit and power: that your faith might not stand on the wisdom of men but on the power of God.' (*I Cor.* 2, 4-5).

He it is who consecrates a man as a witness unto Christ:

> 'But you shall receive the power of the Holy Ghost coming upon you and you shall be witnesses unto Me in Jerusalem, and in all Judea and Samaria, and even unto the uttermost part of the earth.' (*Acts* 1, 8).

He it is who probes and hallows the hearts of men; to whom it is forbidden to lie under pain of punishment:

> 'Ananias why hath Satan tempted thy heart, that thou shouldst lie to the Holy Ghost?' (*Acts* 5, 3).

He it is who inspires the boldness of the apostles:

> 'And the Spirit said to Philip: Go near and join thyself to this chariot.' (*Acts* 8, 29).

and again:

> 'And the Spirit of the Lord took away Philip: and the eunuch saw him no more.' (*Acts* 8, 39).

He it is who quickens the martyrs:

> 'But he (Stephen) being full of the Holy Ghost, looking up steadfastly to heaven, saw the glory of God and Jesus standing on the right hand of God.' (*Acts* 7, 55).

He it was who led Peter to the house of Cornelius:

> '. . . the Spirit said to him: Behold three men seek thee. Arise, therefore: get thee down and go with them doubting nothing.' (*Acts* 10, 19-20).

He it was who chose out the apostles:

> 'And as they were ministering to the Lord and fasting, the Holy Ghost said unto them: Separate me Saul and Barnabas, for the work whereunto I have taken them.' (*Acts* 13, 2).

He is the joy of the persecuted and their surety:

> 'And the disciples were filled with joy and with the Holy Ghost.' (*Acts* 13, 52).

He it was who presided over all decisions affecting the future of the infant Church; indeed the apostles prefaced their directives with these words:

> 'For it hath seemed good to the Holy Ghost and to us to lay no further burden upon you. . . .' (*Acts* 15, 28).

He mapped out the apostles' route, guided them and protected them:

> 'And when they had passed through Phrygia and the country of Galatia, they were forbidden by the Holy Ghost to preach the word in Asia. And when they were come into Mysia, they attempted to go into Bithynia; and the Spirit of Jesus suffered them not.' (*Acts* 16, 6-7).

and again St. Paul says:

> 'And now behold, being bound in the Spirit, I go to Jerusalem: not knowing the things which shall befall me there: Save that the Holy Ghost in every city witnesseth to me saying: that bonds and afflictions wait for me at Jerusalem. But I fear none of these things. . . .' (*Acts* 20, 22-4).

See how consciously the early Church manifested and lived by her faith in the Holy Spirit. It governed St. Paul's whole attitude and was the cause of his shocked astonishment, when at Ephesus to his question: 'Have you received the Holy Ghost since you believed?' the disciples replied: 'We have not so much as heard whether there be a Holy Ghost.' St. Paul could hardly believe his ears: 'In what then were you baptized?' (*Acts* 19, 2-3), he asked incredulously.

Unfortunately that question might well be repeated to many a contemporary Christian. Do they know that they have been baptized with water and Fire and that it is a consuming Fire which through them should spread and reach all men?

The Promise of the Legion, addressed as it is wholly to the Paraclete, is designed to encourage in us worship of the Third Person, and to awaken in us some realization of Him as the soul of our souls, the breath of our breath, closer to us than we are to ourselves. It is meant to make each one exclaim before Him as Claudel did on discovering God:

> 'Behold of a sudden Thou art become a Person for me!'

So speaks an obedient son, eager for God's plan, who longs to open wide his soul for God's love to fill it, for the Acts of the Apostles to be continued.

As a conclusion to this explanation the moving confidence made by Cardinal Mercier at the end of his life, could not be omitted. 'I will tell you,' he wrote, 'one secret of holiness and happiness. If everyday for five minutes you can silence your imagination, shut your eyes and ears to the sights and sounds of the world and withdraw into yourself and there, within the sanctuary of your baptized soul, which is the temple of the Holy Ghost, talk to Him thus:

> O Holy Spirit, soul of my soul, I adore You.
> Enlighten me, guide me, strengthen me, comfort me.
> Tell me what I should do, give me your orders;
> I promise that I will submit to all that You desire of me
>   and accept all You allow to happen to me,
> Grant me only to know your will.

If you do this your life will be happy, calm, and full of consolation, even in the midst of trouble, for grace to the measure of your difficulties will be given you, imbuing you with strength to bear them, and you will arrive at heaven's gate laden with merits.

This submission to the Holy Spirit is the secret of holiness.'

4. Deference to the Action of God.

The promise is addressed, then, to the Holy Ghost. And what do we say to Him at the very beginning of this dialogue between Him and our soul? It opens, as one would expect, with a prayer: a prayer reminding us of and continuing in our hearts the reverent adoration that was Mary's, as the angel told her of the coming of the Spirit. So do we tell Him of our unworthiness of the mission He will entrust to us:

> 'Desiring to be enrolled this day as a Legionary of Mary,
> Yet knowing that of myself I cannot render worthy service,
> Do ask of Thee to come upon me and fill me with Thyself,
> So that my poor acts may be sustained by Thy power and
> Become an instrument of Thy mighty purposes.'

We offer to the Holy Spirit our emptiness, knowing full well that it is an attribute of God to create something out of nothing and that all self-sufficiency offends Him.

We bring to Him awareness of our wretchedness, frank acknowledgement of our weakness, our frequent cowardice and unfaithfulness.

With the Church we are ready to repeat to the Holy Spirit:

> Veni, Pater pauperum . .
> Lava quod est sordidum
> Riga quod est aridum
> Sana quod est saucium
> Flecte quod est rigidum
> Fove quod est frigidum
> Rege quod est devium. (5)

No equivocation is possible. It is for Him to fill our empty hands and for us to pass on that which He has placed in them. It is for Him to flood our souls with His gifts; for us to pass on each grace received, each light, each inspiration. It is for Him to give us plentiful nourishment; for us to share it with our brethren. It is for Him to invade us as a great river carves its bed in the hard rock, so as to spread out over the plain beyond; our part is to offer Him a soul open to His action, stripped of our human outlook, divested of self.

His part is to continue in us the outpouring of grace that flowed into the soul of Mary when, overshadowing her He began through her the Redemption of the world. It is for us to carry on the Marian mystery.

Such an attitude is far removed from one of vainglory in carrying on the apostolate, and from those reformers who bring us their ready-made systems to which God's action is to be made to conform. As if we could possibly understand the ways of the love of God!

'My thoughts,' God says, 'are not your thoughts and My ways are not your ways.'

To those who dare to require of God an account of His actions, has He not given, for all time, the final answer?

'Who is this that wrappeth up sentences in unskilful words? Gird up thy loins like a man. I will ask thee, and answer thou Me. Where wast thou when I laid the foundations of the earth? Tell Me if thou hast understanding. Who hath laid the measures thereof, if thou knowest? Or hath stretched the line upon it? Upon what are its bases grounded? Or who laid the corner stone thereof, when the morning stars praised Me, together and all the sons of God made a joyful melody? ... Didst thou since thy birth command the morning, and shew the dawning of the day its place? ... Hast thou entered into the depths of the sea, and walked in the lowest parts of the deep? ... Hast thou considered the breadth of the earth? Tell Me if thou knowest all things?' (*Job* 38, 2-18).

No, most certainly we do not know. We can only bow down before God's actions as we do before His presence. If God does us the unhoped for honour of needing us, He alone knows the goal and can chart the roads and paths that lead to it. He who would be an apostle must remember that of himself he cannot render worthy service, neither should he venture into unknown country without a map.

In dealing with souls we must bear these things in mind, Above all we must remember them in time of difficulty when our faith is put to the test, when we are tempted to complain to God about our failures. We walk in darkness. It may happen that we stake everything to save a soul and that, so far as we can see, it remains hermetically sealed against grace. And it may also happen that someone else, whom we have not sought, may cross our path and with hardly an effort on our part, may find the way home. We may use such weighty arguments to convince the doubting and fail to rouse a single echo. But perhaps a phrase tossed lightly off in passing, a phrase we do not even remember, may stamp itself upon the heart of someone we scarcely know and lead him to God. Experience of the apostolate teaches us that the grace of God cannot be measured by our scale of values or our human yardstick. We must worship God in His darkness and love Him in His apparent refusals which run counter to our plans. Our apostolic faith must be a constant pursuit of God through all the misrepresentations, denials and attempts to abolish Him. Some day we shall understand the reason for these meanderings and why this enduring patience has been required of us. At present we see human lives from one side, but when we see the side facing Heaven we shall see, as on a tapestry reversed, that all those threads were not entangled together by chance: we shall appreciate the purpose of all that interweaving. Till then our apostolic efforts must be made in darkness, like the activity of God Himself. Hence the Legion expects its soldiers at the outset to recognize their own poverty and nothingness. Thus does it set them in a state of apostolic grace. When I call myself a sinner then it is that God calls me friend. Not until I acknowledge that I am an unprofitable servant can He use me without hesitation, gladly, as 'an instrument of His mighty purposes.'

CHAPTER II.

OUR LADY

BUT I KNOW THAT THOU, WHO HAST COME TO REGENERATE THE WORLD IN JESUS CHRIST, HAST NOT WILLED TO DO SO EXCEPT THROUGH MARY.

1. *The Partnership of the Holy Ghost with our Blessed Lady.*

CHRISTIANITY, we said, is the joining of two loves in Jesus Christ. The Promise repeats this and, with a clarity that is in itself a profession of faith, associates the Holy Spirit and Our Lady.

The Holy Ghost: the love of God stooping down to us.

Our Lady: human love—the purest in all creation—going up to God.

Jesus Christ: the bond of the union, the meeting-place of a twofold love.

We have to understand what this union between the Holy Spirit and His instrument, the most blessed Virgin, means in terms of Christian practice. We have also to discover how far Christ is the fruit of this mutual love.

At the centre of the Catholic creed we find these words: 'and was incarnate by the Holy Ghost of the Virgin Mary.' As the priest says these words at the altar he kneels down to profess his faith in this mystery of mysteries.

It is a simple enough statement, apparently, but one pregnant with incalculable consequences, whose comprehension the Church has never completed, whose fruitfulness she has never exhausted. Who among us has not experienced at certain times, joys too strong to be borne all at once and too extreme to be fully realized? The manifestations of the love of God are depths of this kind:

they must be ceaselessly studied, and lived, for us to see clearly their ineffable blessings and for the extent of their magnificence to be realized. More than all others the mystery of the Incarnation is a revelation ever the same, yet ever new.

In the following pages we wish to linger respectfully over what is, so to say, the heart of this mystery: the meeting of the Holy Ghost with Mary. We do not desire to repeat the Gospel account of past events, but would try to penetrate the vital effects for our own day of this marvellous union which is the seal of the new and eternal alliance.

'The Holy Ghost shall come upon thee and the power of the Most High shall overshadow thee. . . .' (6)

Is that merely a remote historical fact, complete in itself? Or do these words open up for us and for all future time an unchanging law of God's action in the world? The question is important. To limit the alliance between Mary and the Holy Ghost only to the birth of our Lord is to reduce it to the level of an historical episode which, great as it was, lasted only a few swift moments and then faded into the past. It is to put Mary into the past, but not into the present or the future. Is that what God wished? Or did the Holy Spirit by overshadowing her make her everlastingly fruitful? With the whole Catholic Church, on the contrary, we believe that the union of the Holy Ghost with Mary was effected for all time, that thenceforth the alliance was indissoluble and that still today our Lord goes on being born invisible in souls *de Spiritu Sancto ex Maria Virgine*.

We believe it for a reason which is itself a mystery, rooted in the depths of the divine economy; for in a very real sense, which will be made clearer later on, Mary and the Church are one. So much so that to be born 'of the Spirit and of Mary' is tantamount to being born 'of the Spirit and of the Church,' and that the baptism which begets us unto life is the fruit, though in a different way, of this twofold and unique maternity.

2. *The Faithfulness of the Alliance.*

Should one be surprised that God is thus faithful to the order that He has established. This would be to forget that the gifts of God are without repentance, (*Romans* 11, 29), to ignore the fact that all our supernatural life is derived from the mystery of the Incarnation and that in a spiritual but very real way Mary conceived us when the Spirit of the Most High overshadowed her. It would be to understand nothing of God's loyalty to Himself, of which the Scriptures throughout the old alliance give us the most touching proofs. Cannot those solemn promises which God made to His chosen people, of whom Mary was to be the flower and the crown, be applied to the union of the Holy Ghost with Mary?

> 'And I will espouse thee to Me for ever: and I will espouse thee to Me in justice and in judgment and in mercy and in commiserations. And I will espouse thee to Me in faith.' (*Osee* 2, 19-20).

or again this other pledge of Jaweh:

> 'Neither will I profane my covenant: and the words that proceed from my mouth I will not make void.
> Once I have sworn by my holiness: I will not lie unto David. His seed shall endure for ever.
> And his throne as the sun before Me, and as the moon perfect for ever: and a faithful witness in heaven.' (*Psalm* 88, 35-8)

The embassy of the angel to Mary was not limited to promising a transitory visit of the Holy Ghost, a momentary outpouring, restricted solely to the birth of that Son who was to be called Jesus because He was to be the Saviour. The mystery of the Incarnation was to prove to be of far greater extent and its magnificence bounded only by the span of centuries. Mary understood this so well that in her Magnificat she did not fear to utter this triumphant prophecy: 'All generations shall call me blessed.' She knew that in her the history of the world was set in motion.

Mary was to be she whom God raised up 'that David might not be deceived.' She was to be the 'throne established for ever.' She was to be mother of men by the same token that she is mother of God. Through her the Spirit becomes fruitful externally. She will always be the instrument associated with His sanctifying action. For that reason the Holy Ghost came upon her, solely for that reason.

Perhaps we are not sufficiently aware that Mary is God's new creation, a world apart, more marvellous than all other worlds, and that the Spirit which hovered over the waters at the beginning of time is but a remote type of that Virtue which came down upon her.

Once the mystery of the Mystical Body, the union of the Head and members, has been understood, there can no longer be dissociation of what God desires to be one. *Generatio Christi*, says St. Leo, in one of those concise phrases which were his secret, *origo est populi christiani et natalis capitis natalis est corporis* (*Sermon* 26, P.L. 54, 213). 'The generation of Christ is the origin of the Christian people, the birth of the Head is also that of the body.' We have not yet finished elucidating the corollaries of this fundamental dogma. Our generation is recovering increasingly, thank God, the meaning of the mystery of the mystical body. But there is no doubt that it is not yet fully aware of the deep significance that this doctrine confers on the motherhood of Mary. Fr. Doncoeur's remark is well-known: 'This generation, nourished on dogma and the Eucharist, will do great things; but it has yet to discover the Blessed Virgin.'

We also believe that this is the call of the times. But Mary will not be discovered so long as her twofold and unique motherhood, which brings forth the Head and the members, remains unrecognized, so long as the activity of Mary is not associated with that of the Holy Spirit, until it is seen as one action only, the action of the Holy Ghost through Mary. We must re-read and meditate on the words of Blessed Pius X in his memorable encyclical *Ad diem illum* (February 2, 1904):

'... In the chaste womb of the Virgin when Jesus took mortal flesh, He took to Himself also a spiritual body formed of all those who were to believe in Him; and it can be said that, carrying Jesus in her womb, Mary carried also all those whose lives were to be included in His life.

'All of us, then, who are united to Christ are, as the Apostle said, "members of His body, of His flesh and of His bones" (*Ephesians* 5, 30) and should think of ourselves as the fruit of the Virgin's womb, whence we were to issue one day in the likeness of a body attached to its head. It is for this reason that, in a spiritual and mystical sense, we are called the sons of Mary, and that she is, on her side, mother of us all, mother after the Spirit, but the true mother, nevertheless, of the members of Jesus Christ, that we ourselves are.' ([7])

All devotion to Mary which ignores or minimizes this mystery will remain a purely sentimental devotion, thin and anaemic. Cut off from its roots, it will be as a hothouse flower and not an open-air plant. It will be at the mercy of the slightest wind instead of being 'like a tree which is planted near the running waters, which shall bring forth its fruit in due season. And his leaf shall not fall off....' (*Ps.* 1, 3).

The universal motherhood of Mary has its roots in the Incarnation itself. That is the point to which we must continually return. For the Incarnation, in a certain sense, already contains the Redemption. He who is born comes into the world only to die in sacrifice. Unlike all the sons of men, He did not die because He was born; He was born in order to die. He was born priest and victim of the redemptive sacrifice. Our mothers bring forth sons who may one day become priests. For them the priestly dignity is a free gift, not theirs by right of nature. Mary, on the contrary, is the mother of Jesus, who was born a priest; He is the Lamb of God by birth.

Moreover, the maternity of Mary is completed through the mystery of the Redemption. Mary is not our mother in a manner of speaking, metaphorically, or by a purely legal fiction. She is our mother in the full sense, because she co-operated with Jesus, in transmitting to us supernatural life. (8)

Not only is she our true mother, but her spiritual motherhood incomparably surpasses ordinary motherhood. It transmits to us a divine life, an eternal life which makes us members of Christ and children of God. It implies more costly sacrifices: the oblation of Jesus delivering Himself up to death. It exacts more prolonged care: a continuous pregnancy, from the time of our baptism until we enter into heaven. It is accompanied by a motherly tenderness of incomparable magnitude. 'If the hearts of all mothers were put together,' said the Curé d'Ars, 'they would form a block of ice in comparison with hers.' Tertullian said of God that no one is father as He is Father: *tam Pater nemo*. It might be said also of our Lady that no one is mother as she is mother: *tam Mater nemo*. This will be better understood, we hope, when in the chapter devoted to it, we deal with the relationship between Mary and the Church.

In the spiritual life it is a great good fortune when Mary and the Holy Spirit, who have been joined together by God, are not separated. For Mary without the Holy Spirit is but a shadow. The Holy Ghost without Mary is often a remote inaccessible God who is consequently ignored. Christians today need to rediscover the third Person. If they truly believe in this life-giving union they will attain to it, to the greater glory of the Holy Spirit and the joy of Mary.

3. *The Holy Ghost forming Christ in us.*

As soon as the meaning of this indissoluble alliance is understood it becomes clear that the Holy Ghost and, in her place, Mary, cannot fail to unite us to Jesus Christ.

But I know that Thou who hast come to regenerate the world in Jesus Christ, hast not willed to do so except through Mary.

These words show us the function of the Holy Spirit and His unique mission which is to regenerate the world in Jesus Christ. He comes as the Messenger of the Son, prolonging and completing the Son's task. *De meo accipiet,* said Jesus; 'He shall receive of mine.' And elsewhere: 'I have yet many things to say to you: but you cannot bear them now. But when He, the Spirit of truth, is come, He will teach you all truth. For He shall not speak of Himself: but what things soever He shall hear, He shall speak. And the things that are to come, He shall shew you. He shall glorify me: because He shall receive of mine and shew it to you. All things whatsoever the Father hath are mine. Therefore I said that He shall receive of mine and shew it to you.' (*John* 6, 12-5).

Christ, merited all for us through His passion which saved the world, but applied it all to us through the Holy Spirit. The Holy Spirit—that Spirit of life which quickens us—comes to enlighten from within the words of the Master, to guide us in the understanding of the Word, to unseal the closed eyes, to open the ears of the spiritually deaf, to introduce us to 'all truth.' It is not His mission to add any new element to the revelation of Christ.

That statement effectively debars the craving for private revelations for which our contemporaries are avid because their faith is weak. It is not the role of the Holy Spirit to bring a new revelation into the world. Revelation ended with the death of the last apostle and the sole mission of the Church is to keep the deposit intact—*depositum custodi.*

The *Didache,* a book which goes back to the origins of Christianity, is merely expressing a theme familiar to everyone when it puts into the mouth of the apostles who are supposed to be speaking these words: 'If someone comes to you with the teaching which is ours, receive him; if he teaches other things, receive him not.' It must be inferred, therefore, that no revelation, however worthy of respect, made by God to a privileged soul or souls, can introduce any real novelty into the fundamentals of our religion nor, *a fortiori*, monopolize it. No one has given stronger expression to this traditional rule of the Church than St. John of the Cross, a mystic if ever there was one. With rare eloquence he puts souls on their guard against this thirst for novelty and, centuries later, repeats in his own fiery and ardent fashion the still valid precept of the *Didache*. We should like here to quote certain passages from *The Ascent of Mount Carmel*. They express admirably the reasons why, since Christ, all, supplementary, partial revelations have no *raison d'etre* in the Church of God.

'The principal reason why, in the law of Scripture, the enquiries that were made of God were lawful, and why it was fitting that the prophets and priests should seek visions and revelations of God, was because at that time faith had no firm foundation, neither was the evangelical law established: and thus it was needful that they should enquire of God and that He should speak whether by words or by visions and revelations or whether by figures and similitudes or by many other ways of impressing His meaning. For all that He answered and spake and revealed belonged to the mysteries of our faith and things touching it or leading to it. And, since the things of faith are not of man, but are of the mouth of God Himself, God Himself reproved them because they enquired not at His mouth in their affairs, so that He might answer, and might direct their affairs and happenings toward the faith, of which at that time they had no knowledge, because it was not yet founded. But now that the faith is founded in Christ, and, in this era of grace, the evangelical law has been made manifest, there is no reason to enquire of Him in that manner, nor for Him to speak or to answer as He did then. For, in giving us, as He did, His Son, which in His Word—and He has no other—He spake to us all together, once and for all, in this single Word, and He has no occasion to speak further.

'And this is the sense of that passage with which St. Paul begins, when he tries to persuade the Hebrews that they should abandon those first manners and ways of converse with God which are in the law of Moses, and should set their eyes on Christ alone, saying: *Multifariam multisque modis olim Deus loquens patribus in Prophetis: novissime autem diebus istis locutus est nobis in Filio.* And this is as though he had said: That which God spake of old in the prophets to our fathers, in sundry ways and divers manners, He has now, at last, in these days, spoken to us once and for all in the Son. Herein the Apostle declares that God has been, as it were, dumb, and has no more to say, since that which He spake aforetime, in part, to the prophets, He has now spoken altogether in Him, giving us the All, Which is His Son.

'Wherefore he that would now enquire of God, or seek any vision or revelation, would not only be acting foolishly, but would be committing an offence against God, by not setting his eyes altogether upon Christ, and seeking no new thing or aught beside. And God might answer him after this manner, saying: If I have spoken all things to thee in My Word, which is My Son, and I have no other word, what answer can I now make to thee, or what can I reveal to thee which is greater than this? Set thine eyes on Him alone, for in Him I have spoken and revealed to thee all things, and in Him thou shalt find yet more than that which thou askest and desirest. For thou askest locutions and revelations, which are the part; but if thou set thine eyes upon Him, thou shalt find the whole; for He is My complete locution and answer, and He is all My vision and all My revelation; so that I have spoken to thee, answered thee, declared to thee and revealed to thee, in giving Him to thee as thy brother, companion and master, as ransom and as reward. For since that day when I descended upon Him with My Spirit on Mount Tabor, saying: *Hic est filius meus dilectus, in quo mihi bene complacui, ipsum audite* (which is to say: "This is My beloved Son, in Whom I am well pleased; hear ye Him"), I have left off all these manners of teaching and answering, and I have entrusted this to Him. Hear Him; for I have no more faith to reveal, neither have I any more things to declare.' (Book II, Chap. XXII).

This reminder of Catholic tradition is not intended as a denial of private revelations, nor as a belittling of their benefit; it is meant to allot them their right place in the doctrinal scheme and to emphasize how far the Holy Ghost continues and, if one dare to say it, effects Christ.

For that is really His role. His mission is one of vital importance. The treasure has been secured: our Saviour's Blood is the price, paid once for all, of all Redemption. But this Blood must become as dew, falling drop by drop upon souls, to effect in them what may be called *Redemption accepted*. It is the Spirit who makes saints. He it is who irrigates the Church and pours out upon it this infinitely precious Blood. He propels and regulates the circulation of this Blood, like the heart in man's body. He received it to make it bear fruit and in order to effect in us that return to God which is the very purpose of our life. He came down upon the apostles in the cenacle—and in all times upon all the baptized —so that Christ might be born and grow to His full stature in them. He is the secret of growth in Christ, the breath of His mouth, the consequence of His Redemption.

Seated in glory at the right hand of the Father, Christ communicates Himself to us but only through the action of the Holy Spirit. The Paraclete who presided over the birth of our Lord—*spiritus sanctus superveniet in te*—who drew Him into the desert for forty days—*ductus est in desertum a Spiritu*—who led Him to His death—*oblatus est per Spiritum*—continues in us His unique work. Having produced the masterpiece He raises up copies, unfolding all the wealth won for the Body of Christ who is His fullness.

All this is the pure traditional doctrine of the Church, the common heritage of all generations of Christians: he who would live in Christ must open his heart to the Spirit; he who receives the Spirit is united to Christ.

The subject has been explained in the following way by an experienced theologian, E. Tobac: 'The Holy Spirit . . . unites us intimately with Christ because He is, at one and the same time, the Spirit of Christ (*Rom.* 8, 9); He makes us members of Christ, we in Christ and Christ in us. This connection between Christ glorified and the Holy Ghost is so close that the Apostle made no distinction between the two. To live in Christ and to live in the Spirit are one and the same reality, and the in-dwelling of Christ in the soul, is not distinct from the in-dwelling of the Spirit. (*Rom.* 7, 9-11). It would, of course, be wrong to conclude that Christ and the Paraclete are identical persons, but it is a valid inference that the action, in the soul, of Christ glorified is inseparable from that of the Spirit, or more properly, that this action is effected only through the Spirit. The risen Christ communicates to His faithful, the divine Spirit which He Himself possesses in full measure. He is, as it were, the trustee, and in the highest sense of the word, the bestower of the divine Pneuma. He disposes of Its power and Its life. In a word, He wields the dictatorship of the Spirit. ([9])

4. *Our Lady forming Christ in us.*

With an equal assurance we add this: he who desires to live in Christ must open his heart to Christ's Mother.

For what was said above of Christ and the Holy Spirit is true, proportionally speaking and at her own level, of Mary. She, too, will not be separated from her Son. With all her being she reaches out to Him. All devotion to Mary leads to Jesus, as a river flows into the sea. Mary's sole and constant thought is contained in the words she spoke to the servants at Cana: 'Whatsoever He shall say unto you, do ye.' She has no other message. At every one of her appearances throughout the course of history, in one way or another, has been heard the echo of this one sentence which betrays the secret of her soul. She is not only Christocentric, she is the foremost Christian.

The saints, lacking our diffidence, have sung of this fusion of the souls of Mother and Son: 'Jesus, heart of Mary, have pity upon us,' is a familiar invocation of St. John Eudes, who did not consider it daring. Mary, to a higher degree than St. Paul or any other saint, can testify: 'It is not I who live, but Christ who lives in me.' Between her and Him is established an ineffable exchange, a sort of spiritual transfusion. As Fr. Neubert wrote: 'Mary gave to Jesus His humanity, Jesus gave to Mary an ever increasing participation in His divinity; the substance of Mary made and nourished the substance of Jesus, the love of Jesus formed and raised to its own likeness the love of Mary: the blood of Mary circulated in the body of Jesus, the grace of Jesus circulated in the soul of Mary: of her own life she gave to her Son, of His own life He gave to His mother.' [10]

All her mediation, therefore, tends to make other Christs of us, modelling in us, trait by trait, the image of Jesus. With all her being she is Mother of Jesus, a motherhood operative in us. [11]

Neither the Holy Ghost nor Mary confine their actions to themselves. The Holy Spirit is from the very depth of His own being, the gift of self. He is wholly directed towards the Father and the Son, as the Father and the Son are turned towards Him. For the Holy Ghost does not proceed from the Father as if His were solely a self-love, nor from the Son as if He were turned back towards Himself. He proceeds from the unique impulse of the One towards the Other. He is the fruit of their mutual love. And in His turn, He is not enclosed in His own perfection, but bears Himself towards them as in an ecstasy of admiration and recognition, equal to that which He admires and receives. On the same inter-communication in the Blessed Trinity, we may follow the thought of the Greek Fathers, who see divine life coming from the Father, through the Son, in the Spirit. Mary, the creature closest to God, participates more than anyone else in this divine outpouring. She belongs to Christ—*nos autem Christi*—to an unfathomable degree. She is entire submission to Him, a clear transparency.

> Riguardo omai nella faccia ch'a Cristo
> Piu s'assomiglia: che la sua chiarezza
> Sola ti puo disporre a veder Cristo.

'Behold now,' sang Dante, 'the face most like Christ's because its brightness alone can prepare you to see Christ.' ([12])

Why is it that our Christians so often persist in thinking of her as a barrier. The more a soul belongs to God, the closer is it united to God. The more a soul is united to God, the more it unites other souls to Him. Our reservations and diffidence in loving Mary fully for fear of showing insufficient reverence to our Lord, prove our fundamental misunderstanding of what she is. 'It is the role of the Blessed Virgin to lead us surely to Jesus Christ, just as it is the role of Jesus Christ to lead us surely to the eternal Father,' wrote St. Louis Marie de Montfort. ([13])

Here we are at the heart of the mystery of God; it upsets all our narrow systems, our timid calculations and wrecks our neatly-made divisions and compartments; we enter a world of mutual sincerity, of absolute disinterestedness and of luminous communion. ([14])

This is the domain of the Mother of God. That is why Blessed Pius X was able to write: 'There is no more certain or quicker way to unite men to Jesus Christ than Mary, and to obtain through Jesus Christ that perfect adoption of sons which makes us holy and without stain before God. . . . No one in the world has known Jesus as she has, no one is a better master or better guide to the knowledge of Jesus. It follows from this . . . that in uniting men to Jesus no one is of greater value than she.' ([15])

In proportion as our union with Mary increases, not only

will she put into our hearts this or that disposition which she has taken from Jesus, but she will give us her own heart with which to love Him. This is her only thought and her only purpose. To give Jesus to every soul and to the whole world is still the only ambition of this incomparable mother. Let us unite ourselves with her: her limitless love for Jesus will become ours. We shall thus reach a transformation of the soul, an identification with Christ, which will make us think, feel, act and will as He does. Then, and only then, will Mary's task be completed when she can say (with greater justice than St. Paul): 'My little children, of whom I am in labour again, until Christ be formed in you.' (*Gal.* 4, 19). That labour will be no other than our birth into heaven.

CHAPTER III.

MARIAN MEDIATION

I KNOW THAT WITHOUT HER WE CANNOT KNOW OR LOVE THEE; THAT IT IS BY HER, AND TO WHOM SHE PLEASES, WHEN SHE PLEASES, AND IN THE QUANTITY AND MANNER SHE PLEASES, THAT ALL THY GIFTS AND VIRTUES AND GRACES ARE ADMINISTERED.

1. *The Mediation of Mary ascending towards God.*

WE COME now to the statement of Mary's mediation.

It is an ascending mediation: Mary leads us to the Holy Ghost to know Him and to love Him.

It is also a descending mediation: Mary distributes to man the graces of the Holy Ghost.

Reverently we must examine this twofold mystery which forms but one.

We must consider Mary turned towards God.

Her answer to the angel, we said, was made on behalf of mankind. She is—after the love of the Incarnate Word—the purest and the only spotless love, rising up from earth to meet divine Love.

Mary, the Answer to God.

With every fibre of her being she is the *fiat mihi secundum verbum tuum* that her lips pronounced. This is her only desire: to be utterly at the disposal of the Holy Spirit, acquiescent to His Will, wholeheartedly collaborating and corresponding with His work. Ungrudgingly she gives herself up to the Holy Ghost.

In her is realised the highest and most intense freedom in

adherence to God. But there must be no mistake about this: this freedom which says 'yes' is, itself, a unique grace. The free and active co-operation of Mary is wholly nourished with, and steeped, in the Love which effects in her 'the will and the deed'; she remains completely receptive to God's action in the very impulse of her freely consenting liberty. It is not she who takes the initiative: it is God who raises her towards Himself, it is God who gives her the unheard of grace of this complete gift of herself.

Maurice Zundel's beautiful verse about God's generosity is fulfilled in her to an infinitely greater degree than in any of us:

> What He gives He gives truly,
> What he demands He gives again,
> What He receives He gives twice.

If our Protestant brothers would only apply this to Mary, their fears and prejudices would disappear. They fear to see us exaggerate her role at God's expense, as though it was not fitting that God, the first Cause, should associate His free creatures with His work, thus giving to secondary causes the power of collaboration in the divine plan, and of thus becoming better. God acts as God, as a God infinitely good, when He makes us sharers of His power, and capable of good. Thus He creates freedom in us and His grace gives us back our freedom. It is the very mystery of love which unites the maximum dependence and self-surrender with the maximum freedom in spontaneous response to an appeal. The part played by Mary in consenting to the Incarnation is, therefore, simultaneously self-surrender and an act of perfect freedom.

Yet it is surely to God's glory that He should call His creature to His service and give Him part in His superabundant generosity, that God in His absolute independence might consent to dependence. Is this a reversal of values? Is it inconceivable that God, by the archangel Gabriel, should require Mary's consent?

Is it beneath Him to await her answer? Is it not rather a device of matchless delicacy. In the Gospels do we not see Jesus submissive to Mary and Mary to Joseph in a rivalry of obedient affection? This inversion of roles and values might throw a little light for us on God's methods.

Never did creature receive more decisive, magnificent or triumphant a grace than Mary. Yet never did human freedom remain more inviolate. The angel bowed before Mary as a sign of God's respect for her. Mary bowed low before Gabriel's message, and her whole being trembled in veneration for God. This *fiat*, a masterpiece of divine grace and human liberty, a mystery of prevenient grace, which surrendered Mary to the will of God is, for reasons never to be equalled, 'the finest transport of an unfettered love.' ([16])

Mary turned to God, striving towards Him with an outburst of humility. . . . We can contemplate her at length: here below nothing, after the Face of Jesus, is more beautiful. This theocentricity is not a fleeting moment in her soul. Henceforward Mary sees only the Holy Ghost, as the bride sees only the bridegroom. We must consider this wonder more deeply.

We are apt to imagine Mary passing from God to man with a twofold movement; as a dispenser of graces plunging both hands into the treasure, and then, turning round and bending towards us. It is not so. The spiritual reality that we are trying to unveil is infinitely more lovely in its perfect unity. Mary is and remains turned towards the Holy Spirit; it is the fundamental attitude of her soul. And it is in Him that she sees us and in Him that she loves us. Mary goes towards men in God without taking her eyes off Him for a single instant. She is like a sky which allows itself to be saturated by the sun for the greater joy of the earth.

In her untroubled ecstasy in the bosom of God, she sees us with all our miseries and loves us, with a love which she receives from Him, at the very root of our being and the source whence we were born. It is a knowledge incomparably more penetrating than any other, a love which reaches to the deepest intimacy, a motherhood which nourishes us drop by drop to maturity.

When we invoke Mary, we bring her ever nearer to the hearth which sets her ablaze, we unite her more closely to her only love. For when we say: 'The Lord is with thee, blessed art thou among women,' she turns joyfully towards Him who is with her and who pours out His blessings upon her. As our poor laboured *Aves* go up to her, Mary transforms them into hymns to God, triumphant doxologies. An inevitable magic, so to say, comes into operation: we say 'Mary' and she says 'God;' and God is pleased to hearken to what she says on our behalf, as if we said it ourselves. Oh wonderful exchange! Mary turned towards God the better to hear and protect us! We are not used to seeing things from this angle. And yet Jesus Himself gives us to understand that in heaven that is the true perspective. Did He not tell us in speaking of the angels who watch over children that they 'ceaselessly look upon the face of the Father who is in heaven,' —*qui vident faciem Patris qui in caelis est*? If the angels, to whose care God has entrusted men on their journey through life, whose responsibility it is to avoid the stones and serpents in their way, perceive in Him the object of their service, what must it be to be face to face as Mary is? She sees God; she feeds on God; she is wholly steeped in God. Her descending mediation cannot be understood if with the ascending mediation this ever active theocentricity is not also grasped.

Mary, Our Reply to God.

But still it is not enough. To look upon Mary turned towards God, adhering to Him solely by the consent she gave, leaves still one more mystery to be revealed. Mary did not give her answer on her own behalf. St. Thomas tells us that her consent was given *loco totius humanae naturae*, 'in the name of all mankind.' ([17]) In her Amen are echoed all the Amens which will ever go up to heaven from earth. What ineffable joy it is to know that in thus abandoning herself to God, Mary carried us with and in herself.(18)

Hers was not merely *an* answer, it was *the* answer of humanity to the love of God. And it is now her motherly task to help us to whatever in us makes for free consent to divine grace, a welcome to the gift of God. It is her part to help us convey our desires and prayers to God. What greater support could we have in seeking grace from the Most High than to be upheld before Him by her of whom it is said *invenisi gratiam*, 'thou hast found favour'? It is for her also to help us to believe in the mystery of the love of God. Her faith will be a refuge for ours. Sheltered in her, as in the tower of David, we shall not falter beneath the weight of a love too great for our insignificance, and we shall dare to believe in the impossible.

Thus with Mary, through Mary, and in Mary, we penetrate, gradually but surely into the mystery of our configuration with Christ Jesus, which is the final fruit of our dependence on His divine Mother.

Under Mary's influence, our birth and growth as Christians are effected with rare gentleness. Our progress is assured. We belong to Mary, but Mary belongs to Christ. There is her whole function. 'It is characteristic of Our Lady,' said Cardinal de Berulle, 'that hers is a pure capacity for Jesus, entirely filled with Jesus.' The same must be said of her mission in our regard: she is simply the motherhood of Jesus prolonged in souls, a mediation solely filled with him. She received the Holy Ghost only that Jesus Christ might be begotten.

*
* *

But if Mary is all that, it follows that she is also for us the means of access to the Holy Ghost.

I know that without her we cannot know or love Thee.

We know already that Mary is a world of wonders that alone can reveal to us the Spirit who plumbs the depths of God. Saint

Louis Marie de Montfort tells us this in admirable terms: 'Mary is the unsurpassed masterpiece of the Most High, whose knowledge and possession He has kept for Himself. ... Mary is the faithful bride of the Holy Ghost, and the sealed fountain to which He alone has access. Mary is the sanctuary and resting-place of the Holy Trinity, where God dwells more gloriously and divinely than in any other place in the universe, not excepting His dwelling among the Cherubim and Seraphim; no creature, however pure it be, may enter there without a great privilege.' [19]

And again: 'Mary is the paradise of God where the Son of God has entered to work His wonders for its protection and His own delight. ... He has made a world for man on his journey, and it is this in which we live; He made a world for the blessed which is paradise. But He has made another for Himself and to this He gave the name of Mary.' [20]

But the converse is also true. If the Holy Ghost alone can give us understanding of Mary, 'without her we cannot know or love Him.' By an extraordinary exchange Mary becomes our introduction to Him; she is the repository of the King's secrets. To approach her means, by the same gesture, to approach Him. No, we must not be afraid to receive Mary: what is born of her is of the Holy Spirit. *Noli timere accipere Mariam. Quod enim in ea natum est de Spiritu Sancto est.*

These words were said to St. Joseph to relieve his anxiety at that moment when the angel counselled him to hesitate no longer. Beyond the concrete circumstances in which these words are set, we may descry something more than advice for that occasion: a secret of life. He who is born of Mary is born of the Holy Ghost. This co-operation, we said, is applicable to all times, and so there should be no hesitation on our part to 'receive Mary.' In opening our hearts to her, we open them to the Holy Ghost; in uniting ourselves to her we unite ourselves with the Holy Ghost.

We can penetrate further into this mystery. There are those famous lines by St. Louis Marie de Montfort: 'When the Holy

Ghost has found Mary, His bride, in a soul, He flies there, He enters there in His fullness, He communicates Himself to that soul abundantly, and to the full extent to which it makes room for His bride. One of the great reasons why the Holy Ghost does not now work conspicuous wonders in the souls of men is because He does not find in them a sufficiently intimate union with His faithful and inseparable Bride. I say inseparable Bride for, since that substantial love of the Father and the Son has espoused Mary to produce Jesus Christ, the Head of the elect, He has never repudiated her because she has always been faithful and fruitful.' ([21])

It could not be said more concisely that Mary is the highway to the Holy Spirit, that her cult is, if one may so put it, entirely 'spiritual,' entirely in relation to Him. Here again we can discover a further aspect of God's infinite mercy and condescension towards the poor weak creatures that we are.

Mary, gracious condescension of God towards our weakness of spirit.

Mary, gracious condescension of God towards our needy hearts.

We can now consider this in detail.

Mary, the Image of the Holy Ghost.

Without her we cannot know Thee. . . .

We are, perhaps, unaccustomed to thinking of Mary as the mirror of the Holy Spirit, *speculum sine macula*, to approaching her as our introduction to Him. Yet the expression seems accurate since Mary is of priceless assistance in raising us to Him. How, indeed, with our limited, clumsy ideas can we understand Him or grasp what He is? It is difficult for our minds, confined to earth as they are, to realize what God the Father is, or God the Son, in spite of the fact that we know what a father is and what a son is here below, and can base an analogy on them as an aid to our weakness. But who will help us to glimpse this mysterious

Holy Spirit whom we can only imagine through the symbol of a dove or of fire?

Could we not find a more exact image, an expression within our comprehension to lead us to Him and act as a sort of interpreter?

We believe that through God's condescension, Mary is a pure and unsullied introduction to the Spirit of all purity and all light. It is not through love of paradox or extravagance that St. Louis Marie de Montfort dares to say that practical ignorance about the Holy Ghost actually originates in neglect of Mary. Their union is a more perfect one than is commonly supposed. We do not claim that all contact with the Holy Spirit presupposes a conscious and intentional recourse to Mary. But, whether or not we have recourse to her consciously, Mary's mediation is what it is, even unknown to us, for such is God's objective plan.

We can consider for a moment the part played by Christ's human nature in introducing us to knowledge of the Person of the Word. For He, too, the Word of God, is far beyond our power of thought, out of our reach, dwelling in inaccessible light. Becoming incarnate, the Word became for us palpable, tangible, comprehensible. All prayer to Jesus straightway reaches the Word, all worship of Jesus goes up to the Word, all that belongs to Jesus belongs to the Word of God.

Would it be bold to seek in this example an analogy, remote no doubt, and deficient in many ways, yet within certain limits of some utility? Any suggestion of a kind of hypostatic union between the Holy Spirit and Mary must be rigorously avoided. But bearing that proviso in mind, is there not, between Him and her, through the free will of God, an operative union in regard to us which makes Mary an instrument directly united to the Spirit which works through her? A theologian like Scheeben hails Mary as the original image of the Church. ([22]) Mary, he says, in her own person, realizes fully the idea of the Church, whose soul is the Holy Ghost. Mary, he says again, is the organ of the Holy

Spirit just as, by analogy, the humanity of Christ is the instrument of the Logos. In truth, she is the powerful instrument of the Paraclete. So we can see how St. Ephrem dared to address Mary in these words: *Post Trinitatem omnium Domina, post Paracletum alia paraclitus.* ([23]) We can also unders and how tradition came to make of the dove—the symbol of the Holy Spirit—the symbol of Mary.

From all this we can conclude that for us poor mortals, Mary is the short cut—that famous short cut promised in so many spiritual books, with their deceptively long ways round—leading in practice, straight to the Holy Ghost. If we love her we love Him. Who serves her serves Him. Who belongs to her belongs to Him. Foolhardy indeed those who would by-pass her the better to reach him. ([24])

And this route is normal when it is known that the ways of God are always accessible and within our reach. Nothing is further from Him than false grandeur. His kingdom is open to children and those who are like them. All that is complex, or esoteric is the antithesis of His wisdom. *Revelasti ea parvulis*: thou hast revealed these things to little ones. We must be able to live this devotion to the Holy Spirit simply, familiarly, in a way that is easy for all. In the Church of God subtle minds have no priority. What God in His spiritual plan wants men to have, He has put within their reach, like air and water and light. Now devotion to the Holy Ghost is not a luxury; it lies at the heart of all Christian life. Mary is the way of access to the Holy Ghost. How much better we can now understand the simplicity of the love and teaching of God. May we, therefore, be introduced by her and led as by the hand.

*
* *

*Mary, the Reflection of the Divine Heart.
Nor love Thee. . . .*

After the humanity of Christ, Mary is God's supreme attempt to convince us of His love. She has nothing that she did not receive from Him. After the human nature of Christ she is the crowning point of His creation. He is the source of all her love and all her care for us.

In Mary God loves us with a love that seems to come within the order of things felt by our hearts. Mary is not only the image of the Holy Spirit, as we have just said, she is an unequalled introduction to the knowledge of the love of God. To acknowledge God without accepting His revelation and active presence in her is a belittling of the God of love, a mutilation of His most positive manifestations. 'Can a woman forget her infant,' said the Lord, 'so as not to have pity on the Son of her womb? And if she should forget, yet will I not forget thee.' And again: 'As one whom the mother caresseth, so will I comfort you. . . .' God chose Mary to keep us in mind of this in a way appropriate to our weakness and adapted to our needs.

To stand aside from her on the pretext of better honouring God is to reject God. It is not possible to know God as He is for us, so long as we do not recognize her whose mission it is to draw us ever closer to His love. How, then, is it possible to grasp this love without seeing her, in her place, as bringing within our reach a revelation of God? Moreover, the saints, who loved Mary with all the fervour that they felt towards God, were not mistaken. And sinners also know it by instinct: in their wretchedness they clutch her motherly hands as their last hope of salvation. It is proved by experience: nothing is lost as long as an *Ave Maria* can be said, as long as one can cling to a fold of Mary's robe. Innumerable accounts of conversions *in extremis* bear witness to the fact that the fringe of her maternal garment is, as it were, the last enveloping of a love which enfolds us.

There are times when it seems difficult to repeat the *Pater* honestly. It contains phrases that call for heroism: 'Thy Will be done . . . forgive us our trespasses as we forgive them that trespass against us.' The *Ave Maria* is, therefore, for many, the last plank of salvation. We can always go to weep out our sorrows to our mother, and say to her 'Pray for us sinners.' The *Ave* leads one insensibly to the *Pater*, much as the ten *Aves* of a decade of the Rosary prepare us to say, with and in Mary, an Our Father less unworthy of God. Mary is the love of God on a level with the sinners and little children that we are. Mary is the love of God which comes within the reach of our weakness, our faltering steps, our fears, our tears.

It is said of Jesus that He loved us to the end: *In finem dilexit eos.* His last deed was to give His mother to St. John, that is, to us. She is the apogee of His love. He could go no farther: *Quid ultra debui facere vineae meae at non feci?* 'What was there that I ought to do more to my vineyard that I have not done to it?' Truly it can be said that all who misunderstand Mary misunderstand the heart of God.

2. Mediation of Mary descending towards Men.

As there is a mediation which goes up, so there is also a mediation coming down from heaven to earth.

The Vexillum of the Legion proudly bears the picture of Mary, Mediatrix of all Graces, bending down towards us, arms wide open, hands glistening with rays of light. Thus did St. Catherine Labouré see Our Lady when, in the rue du Bac, the design for the miraculous medal was revealed to her.

Perpetual Mediation.

The Legion, like the Church, and in the same way as she does, believes 'that it is by her, and to whom she pleases, when she pleases, and in the quantity and manner she pleases, that all thy gifts and virtues and graces are administered.' While it is not yet a defined dogma, the doctrine taught by the ordinary magisterium of the Church and recognized in the feast of May 31, is no longer questioned in substance. We believe that Mary distributes all the graces of God just as we believe that the Holy Ghost is faithful to her whom He chose from among all women.

We reiterate that God could have done without her, just as He need not have created the universe. But by a definite and deliberate choice He willed to come to us through her. As Bossuet so magnificently says: 'It is and will always remain true that, having once received the universal source of all grace through her, through her agency we continue to receive grace appropriate to every state of Christian life. Since her maternal charity contributed so greatly to our salvation in the Incarnation, the universal source of grace, she will continue to contribute to it eternally in all those other operations which are merely dependent upon it.' [25]

God has willed that this dependence should be continual and perpetual. As in the natural order the preservation of the species is assured by a continuing and never failing creation, so the dependence of the soul on the Mother of God is, whether we are aware of it or not, indispensable.

By mention of this active presence of Mary in us, by no means do we intend to attribute to her that indwelling which is the province of God alone. But if God alone dwells within our hearts and permeates them with His grace, Mary is, after Christ, the created instrument which God uses to carry this work into effect, and on this score it can be said that she is in travail within us in her role of constant motherhood. Her influence enfolds us on all sides: we are born of the Holy Ghost and of Mary. To declare her Mediatrix of some graces but not of all, would be a misrepresentation of the faithfulness of God.

Hence, voluntarily to cease to cleave to Mary is to leave hold of life. Such is the order in God's plan. Those who would go to Christ without her, who would seek the child without the mother, show no deference to God's designs. *Invenerunt puerum cum Maria matre ejus.* There is our way. Jesus cannot be found save in the arms of Mary. It is, perhaps, because they have misunderstood Mary that certain Protestants have ceased to recognize even the divinity of Jesus. By thrusting Mary to one side they deny the transcendence of her Son. They have come to think of Christ as the first among men, belonging to the order of mere creatures. They have put Jesus where we put Mary, in the first rank of creation, so true is it that none may with impunity touch the greatness of the Mother of God, and her role of introductress.

A Mediation subordinated to the unique Mediation of Christ.

Noli timere accipere Mariam. We should not be afraid to accept the mystery of this Marian mediation which, basically, is only the motherhood of Mary in its mystical fullness. Nor should we set her aside on the pretext of greater reverence for the sole mediation of Jesus.

Of course we believe with the Church that Christ alone is wholly and absolutely mediator between God and man. But the precise character of Mary's mediation, derived from and subordinate to that of her Son, is to enable us to penetrate deeper into His unique mediation.

We repeat: Mary is not a mediator interposed by Christ to keep men at a distance from Him. 'On the contrary,' as Fr. Mersch put it so excellently, 'She is the means that He adopted so that there should be no distance, and mankind in Him might directly touch God. Thus there is but one Mediator who needs no completion by anything else. But an element of His completeness is assured by His mother. Thus the mediation of Mary is to be found in the first place in that of Christ, and functions in Him: the mediation of Jesus, from the human side is perfect by being Marian. . . .

'Mary's mediation merely expresses and actuates one element of Christ's mediation; the element through which it is adapted to all men a complete gift and entirely accessible; in brief, it is solely the mediation as mother of God, that is the mediation of the God-Man, in so far as having a mother He is fully man. . . . Created as a link, as a perfecting of the bond between God and man, her function is that of liaison.' ([26])

It could not be put in better words: all the glory of Mary lies in this: her motherhood by attesting the truth of the human nature of Jesus, enables Him to be the mediator who has in Himself everything required for the union of man with God. If it is so with Him it is because in her was accomplished the liaison between the two natures of God and man.

What we give to Mary goes most surely directly and wholly to God. And not merely is it given over in its entirety, but it is enriched and increased by the merits of the intermediary. By passing through her hands, our offerings gain new value, and reach the throne of God unsullied. Thence, too, graces are showered down like dew from heaven, with a sweet bounty.

In the light of this doctrine it is easier to understand the hidden meaning of the Gospels when they show us Mary.

It was through her that the Precursor was sanctified and Elizabeth flooded with grace.

It was through her that the shepherds and kings discovered the Messiah.

It was through her that Simeon and Anna held in their arms the Desire of nations.

It was her prayer that produced the first miracle at Cana.

It was through her that mankind at the foot of the cross ratified the sacrifice of Redemption.

It was in union with her that the Holy Ghost was sent down on the apostles at Pentecost, and that the apostolate was begun.

These scattered, unobtrusive events, occurring in the half-light are but the prelude to the first gleams of the Marian dawn, whose shining splendour will increase, until its light fills the whole firmament of the Church.

CHAPTER IV.

UNION WITH MARY

AND I REALISE, THAT THE SECRET OF A PERFECT LEGIONARY CONSISTS IN A COMPLETE UNION WITH HER WHO IS SO COMPLETELY UNITED TO THEE.

1. *The Way of Childhood*: 'In Sinu Matris.'

THERE IS INDEED A SECRET. There are secrets of nature, said St. Louis-Marie de Montfort, but there are also secrets of grace 'so that in a short time, calmly and easily, supernatural acts—to be emptied of self, and filled with God—may ensue. . . .' In a few words this secret is:

A complete union with her who is so completely united to Thee.

This is the vital and practical corollary following upon all that has been said so far. If Mary is what she is we must unite ourselves to her as closely as possible.

All Christians claim Our Lady as their mother. All call themselves her children. But to one's mother one is a child at many different ages. The man who is fortunate enough to live with his mother is always her child. But he has a life of his own: worries, work and trials that he does not share with her. She may die; he goes on living. He is her child, yet he lives outside her life. The more he advances in life, the greater becomes his self-dependence and it is right that this should be so. Is that what is meant by being a child of the most Blessed Virgin?

Obviously it is not; a closer parallel must be found. Is the ideal a child of a few months old in his mother's arms? In this case there is much closer dependence. The child in the cradle cannot take a step without his mother. From her he obtains his food, drop by drop, mouthful by mouthful. Is that the right picture of our dependence upon Mary? Not yet. This child can live if his mother dies tomorrow. He can move and breathe without her. We must not hesitate to go still farther back in the story of a child's dependence upon his mother's care, to when he is in his mother's womb.

The child is never more his mother's than when he dwells within her womb. He lives then in total and absolute dependence on her. His life is hers, he breathes through her.

The Legionary, by uniting himself to Mary in the closest possible way, by agreeing to be always and for ever *in sinu Matris* as we would be always *in sinu Ecclesiae*, is following Gospel teaching exactly. Here figures are inadequate: the spiritual reality defies comparison.

In natural life it is normal for the child to be separated from his mother and grow progressively farther away from her, but in supernatural life, on the contrary, our growth in Christ will make us increasingly dependent upon Mary. All the elect are formed in her, and so remain hidden in her as long as their formation lasts, that is, throughout their life here below. We need a mother, in a special way, during the time of our weakness: grace is the germ of glory, a germ needing protection from contrary winds and storms. We are all, until death, in process of being born. Even the greatest saints are carried by Mary, and her motherhood increases in proportion to their willing dependence.

Paradise itself will come as the glorious conclusion, with the crowning of Mary as eternally Queen of Heaven. ([27])

All this is expressed by the secret to which the Promise alludes. I am called to *a complete union with her who is so completely united to Thee.*

2. Union with Mary, the Way to God.

Furthermore, the consequences of this union are as numerous, as they are hard to express.

United with her, then, it is not I who progress towards God but she. *Ego autem* IN INNOCENTIA MEA *ingressus sum*. Mary is the innocence which I put on, the better to put on Christ and rise towards the Most High. *Exaudisti precem meam* IN MEDIO TEMPLI TUI. God hears the prayer which I offer within this temple which is Mary. *In utero Matris meae exaudisti me*. Because this temple shelters the Holy of Holies, our Lord Jesus Christ.

A wonderful change takes place in our prayers and offerings when we immerse them in Mary. Our gift rises *cum odore suavitatis*, with a new sweet smelling odour, pleasing to God. The voice of Mary, because it is the most faithful echo of the voice of her Son, delights the heart of God. *Sonet vox tua in auribus meis, vox enim tua dulcis* (Cant. 2, 14) 'Let thy voice sound in my ears for thy voice is sweet.'

There is a world of difference between the ordinary devotion to Mary currently practised and the union with her under consideration here. ([28])

Many reverence Mary, address a passing invocation to her, visit her shrines and perform some daily practice in her honour. Few are vowed to her service, abandon their souls to her, and, in fact, live in a state of perpetual consecration to Mary. Again, many are full of admiration for her, endeavour to copy her virtues as an artist attempts to reproduce from outside the characteristics of a model. Yet how few there are who, not content with this fragmentary external copying, live this interior assimilation, this fusion of the soul which exceeds in its spiritual intimacy any description we can give of it. The term 'Metaphysics of the saints' has been used to describe a spiritual life founded upon the dogma of sanctifying grace, enduring and inherent in the soul, in contrast to a life which seems to rely only upon actual and transient grace, because it neglects to emphasize this basic reality. Almost in the same way it might be said that there is a metaphysic of the most Blessed Virgin which alone attains to her in reality and truth. Words may vary in different ages, but we should try to get back behind the words to the great Marian tradition which, with rare insight, called this metaphysical aspect 'the interior of Mary.'

We should pay attention to and consider carefully those wonderful words of M. Olier's, 'The smallest share in the interior of Mary, the slightest participation in her grace is a greater treasure than all the Seraphim and other angels and saints ever say to God. Heaven and earth have nothing approaching this life, this wonderful interior where can be found all the worship, all the praise, all the love of the Church, of men and of angels; and a thousandfold more than all that His whole creation can render to Him. Such are the heights of her grace and holiness. This is why more greater progress is made towards procuring the glory of God, the good of the Church, and personal perfection by union with Mary than by any other practices.'

In all Marian literature we know few texts more significative or fruitful than that. These words must be deeply pondered and put into living practice. This interior of Mary is, in fact, the Ark of the Covenant where the soul may dwell in order to live that spiritual life which is communion with the Holy Ghost. Over this Ark hovered the power of the Most High; there we are, where we should be, to receive its benefits.

It is enough for the soul to live in Mary. As it trustfully abandons itself to its mother, increasingly is it aware of breathing in union with her. The soul closely united to Mary, should frequently call on the Holy Ghost—*Veni Sancte Spiritus*!—and its spiritual growth, its growing in likeness to Christ will go on and be strengthened; union will become continuous.

All this is extremely simple: a secret of grace within the grasp of children.

Union with Mary and the Will of God.

We must go to God in Mary so that Christ may increase. **Why** this apparent way round?

It is the will of God. We must not love Mary merely because we feel an attraction for her. We are fortunate to experience the delight of this attraction, but in any case we depend entirely on the adorable will of God. The primary and basic reason for our love of Mary is that it is God's will.

When shall we learn to love the will of God in itself, and for its own sake? It is enough for us to know that God means to communicate Himself to us through her for our will to unite with His and direct our attitude and our love. To love means to desire to love. That statement protects our love, and places it beyond the reach of our vacillation due to psychological and emotional reasons. Devotion to Mary is a virile quality, springing from and drawing its constancy and strength from the Holy will of God.

Union with Mary and the Holiness of God.

To approach our only Mediator, through Mary, is to acknowledge His unequalled sanctity and to abase ourselves yet more deeply before Him. *Exii a me, Domine, quia homo peccator sum.* 'Depart from me, O Lord, for I am a sinful man.' This spontaneous cry of St. Peter's on seeing Our Lord is an act both of reverence and truth.

God's holiness is so great that we must ceaselessly become more humble, prostrating ourselves lower even than the earth. The practice of Marian mediation brings home to us, ever more clearly, our own fundamental impurity, and God's majesty.

Often we scarcely dare approach Him, we are awkward in His presence. We are deeply conscious of the clumsiness of our prayers, the discordant nature of our praise. In place of our voices we would substitute one pleasing to the heart of God, which rejoices in a prayer that is purified, clear as spring water. We must turn to Mary: she will be the harp accompanying our singing, the precious cup of our libations. God looks upon her with unutterable pleasure, for she is that harp attuned to Christ like no other, is that cup chosen by Him for the offering to Him of the Blood of His Son: *pro nostra et totius mundi salute*—for our salvation and that of the whole world.(29)

Union with Mary and Abandonment to God.

Union with Mary is not only an act of reverence to the holiness of God, it is also by far the easiest method of practising the way of spiritual childhood and abandonment.

The child about to be born worries about neither the past nor the future. It lives for the moment, and only the present moment. It breathes second by second, and is wholly absorbed in the present. At each beat of her heart its mother feeds it with her flesh and blood, although it is unaware of it. It is wrapped in her life-giving tenderness which never fails it. That is a picture of the authentic spiritual life. In the light of this should be read the beautiful treatise by Father de Caussade, S.J., on 'Abandonment to Divine Providence' and the contribution of this Marian way rendering it easy, flexible and complete will be understood. God does not want us to live outside His present will, which enshrines for us all His love. Yesterday is over: leave it to His mercy. Tomorrow is yet to come: trust blindly to His never-failing care. But today is here and is an invitation to surrender ourselves wholeheartedly, to the love of God in action. The soul united with Mary has only to unite itself in her with this sanctifying will. It needs to know no more. Each breath with Mary is a spiritual longing. It is a ceaseless communion under the thousand different forms of present duty to be done. What peace, what security, what surrender! We are so anxious to map out our own road, to plan details, to foresee the morrow, yet none of this is compatible with the spirit of childhood, which leads us to a continual renewal of our surrender to the present will of God. Marvellous results of grace may ensue, for with every instant that the faithful child thus breathes in Mary, a process of purification is taking place. *Posui immaculatam viam meam.* The Marian way is a road without blemish. All that passes through her undergoes a certain transformation and renewal by grace. All our poor motives for our actions are purified, Christ's dispositions imperceptibly become our own: God's glory and God's glory alone becomes the sole ambition of our being.

Practising this Marian dependence we prolong that of Christ during the nine months of His hidden life. The disciple is not better than his master. We must not be afraid to follow Him *quocumque ierit*, along every road He has chosen, and to dwell in the place He made so gloriously His own. So that, thinking of Mary we shall be able to say: *Domine dilexi decorem domus tuae et locum habitationis gloriae tuae.* 'Lord I have loved the splendour of Thy house and the place where Thy glory dwelleth.'

Union with Mary and the Communion of Saints.

United with Mary we enter into Christ and go to God. But we cannot isolate God from the world of the angels, the saints of the Church triumphant and the souls in Purgatory. Heaven is an immense family with which we, the children of God and members of His household, have an invisible though manifold and thrilling relationship. Faith reveals to us the legions of angels as night shows us the myriads of stars. *Et nox illuminatio mea.* A world is unfolded before our dazzled eyes, and links are forged between us and the angels. We feel that we are wrapped round and supported by the thousand bonds of undreamt affection; angels watch our every step, passing up and down above us as in the mysterious vision of Jacob's ladder. But Mary is Queen of the Angels, so, naturally, she introduces us to them. Thus, united with her we can approach Thrones, Powers, Seraphim, Cherubim, Angels and Archangels. We can draw near to them and love them with her heart and give thanks to God for the greatness of their glory. We say the *Deo Gratias* of their paeans of thanks, and the *Gloria* of their inexhaustible worship. She puts us on a level with them. She gives us the right of intimacy with St. Michael, prince of the Heavenly court and guardian of the glory of God, with St. Gabriel, Archangel of the Annunciation and messenger of the love of God, with St. Raphael, Archangel of joy, who watches over the footsteps of travellers, as we are, and contrives for us propitious encounters.

Mary is Queen, too, of the Saints, and introduces us to them. According to the measure of our union with her, we can love them all with her heart, her refinement, her gratitude. For who can love them as she does? Can we have even an inkling of her heart's delight in St. Joseph, or her concern for each one of the Apostles? Our union with her simplifies at once what, by a process of division, we call 'devotions.' Instead of placing side by side veneration of St. Paul or St. Theresa, all these affections in the love of Mary which unites them, are fused into one of pleasing diversity.

We have not, nowadays, enough disinterested devotion to the saints, nor do we—as our forefathers did—make the reading of their lives the food of our admiration. And yet 'God only made the world and disrupted it, in order to make saints.'

Earth ceases to justify its existence the moment the last saint is born to Heaven. Their histories, more thrilling than any adventure story, are the only ones of any decisive value. They are nothing but the continuation of the Incarnation of Jesus, and so remain the work of the Holy Ghost and of Mary. Every saint —from the least known to the most glorious—is born of her and all the graces which have made a saint passed through her hands. In her we can love them with a new heart and a new soul. And the intimacy matures and increases indefinitely with unsuspected and pleasant simplicity. We are co-heirs of Heaven and already we are the sons of the house.

As Queen of Purgatory, Our Lady opens for us the door to the Church suffering. Our prayers, in union with those of Mary Immaculate, can hasten the work of purifying those numberless souls; we can share in her maternal impatience to be for them the gateway to Heaven. All this almost without thinking, quite simply and naturally, because everyone can say 'Her heart and mine are but one.'

Union with Mary is a school where can be learned a proper scale of values and orders of importance. She shows us how to admire God's living riches. She gives us devotion to the saints celebrated on a particular day; they are brought close to us, we share the Church's joy in their feast day, we honour and invoke them. They appear to us as kindly and beneficent, as willing to help. Mary instils into us respect for our guardian angel, our patron saint, the guardian angel of our country, the patron of our parish. She does it because it is the truth, for, better than we, she knows that they are really patrons and not fictions of imagination. And she does it, too, because these numerous mediators reveal to us, like a prism which splits light into its component colours, the light of a sole love of God.

This constant union with Mary, obviously, permeates all our religious life, in its entirety and in its details, and at every level.

It must be acknowledged that the Christian united with Mary has a special way of fulfilling all his duties, even to the very least of them: there is a Marian way of assisting at Mass, giving thanks to God, saying the Divine Office and making the sign of the Cross. Bernadette, taught by Mary to make the sign of the Cross slowly, in the name of the Father and of the Son and of the Holy Ghost, bears witness to this care which overlooks nothing and gives its full value to everything.

3. *Union with Mary, the Way to Men's Hearts.*

Our relations with the earth, no less than our relations with heaven, bear the stamp of our belonging to Mary.

If God must be approached through her, so, too, must mankind. Devotion to Mary is meaningless if it is not apostolic. It is the Legion's great merit to have linked Mary and action so closely. All too frequently devotion to Our Lady is confined within the limits of a *tête à tête* instead of making of this individual devotion the basis of all missionary action just as, in a different category, we should make our personal eucharistic communion the very foundation of our love of the community. That is but a poor and pale reflection of the real thing. For if our devotion to Mary is to be confined to certain practices of devotion behind closed doors, it will be deprived of its sap, and the nourishing soil whereon it grows.

Union with Mary and the Apostolate.

Devotion to Mary properly understood and in the active sense of the word is the same thing as the apostolate, for Mary is and remains she who bears Christ. This separation between a so-called devotion to Mary and action is at the bottom of a certain spiritual sclerosis from which all too many devout souls suffer. It accounts for their lamentable coldness towards her. A partial lack of respect for the truth is always dangerous; not only will Christian devotion suffer, but also apostolic action. It can so easily degenerate into unfruitful activity, sheltering under a distorted and secularized conception of the apostolate.

A whole scale of useful and even indispensable activities has been given this sacred title. A centrifugal movement has increasingly alienated the modern mentality from the apostolate in its primary evangelical meaning. Are we, or are we not, working on the lines of the Acts of the Apostles? Is the apostolate, which we mention primarily, that same passing on of supernatural life to our neighbour who knows it not? Devotion to Mary, divorced from apostolic work, will not save us from activism, but, 'the true devotion,' as it was well understood by St. Louis-Marie de Montfort, will sanctify action, making it apostolic and fruitful. The certain, traditional and beneficial method is the one which combines this 'true devotion' with action and so mutually invigorates both.

For the religious, evangelical and direct apostolate, with which we are here concerned, is a spiritual motherhood. It can take many forms, whether collective or individual. Every possible influence is used to approach souls; in the last resort, to be an apostle means to give birth to Christ or to cause Him to grow, in our brothers. In a very special manner it means carrying on the work of Mary herself. Union with her, therefore, is the inevitable rule. So the Legionary approaches men, conscious that not he, but she through him, approaches them. He has been told that 'efforts not under Mary's presidency are like oil without lamps.' (Manual). This is why the first thing he sees at his weekly meeting is a statue of Our Lady surrounded by her Legionaries. She is waiting for them. She confides to them her maternal anxieties and shows them her children who are in danger. She calls upon them to share in her work: she goes with them on the way from door to door.

Through every Legionary, on a visit of the apostolate, she can say: *Ecce sto ad ostium et pulso.* 'Behold I stand at the door and knock.' Here I am knocking at the door of this house of this soul. Just as she did of old in narrow streets of Bethlehem, on Christmas Eve, so does she now. She is there, present, active, more motherly than ever. Generally the Legionary has no outward evidence of her presence and goes forward in the darkness of faith, knowing that she is with him. Occasionally, however, he can point to a presence far more penetrating and effective than his own, a successful result enhancing and indeed surpassing, the effect of his clumsy words. She is always on the watch and makes use of everything 'like a careful housekeeper,' but she needs our steps, our words and our weariness. She expects us to love our brother in the sweat of our brow. Legionaries know what that means and do not hesitate to knock at some unwelcoming door, ten, twenty, fifty times; courteously to return again, again and again; to hold on in face of wind and tide. They know that the Master promised that it shall be opened to whomsoever shall knock, though they remember that Our Lord did not state the exact number of knocks required.

How mysterious are the ways of grace! We make some gesture, we utter some words; we think we have succeeded, and nothing happens. Perhaps our tentative advance meets with an unfriendly reception, repeated maybe ten or even twenty times. Then one fine day, at some unexpected turning, grace suddenly comes into action and a conversion is set on foot. Only then is it realised that no word was, in fact, useless: like a battering-ram they hammered at the seemingly impregnable walls. We only noticed the return-shock, and this shock can be painful, until the breach opened almost without effort. Mary, mother in the highest sense of the word, to a greater degree than any other mother, has received the divine gift of inexhaustible love; that is why Marian apostolic action is enduring patience, solicitous care which ceases not to hope and wait. Has a mother ever been seen who would submit with good grace to her child going astray? That is why the Legionary, too, can never accept defeat, still less defeatism. For that would mean abjuring Mary, standing by, arms folded, unconcernedly watching the shipwreck of souls.

Union with Mary and Charity.

But that is not all. Not only are devotion to Mary and apostolic self-sacrifice identical, but union with Mary endows our spiritual charity with a quite distinctive character of its own. It has been said that there is such a thing as 'legionary charity.' Not, of course, that it differs in any radical way from plain charity: for all men it is always rooted in love for God Himself, love for our neighbour in God for His sake. But just as it is possible to speak of 'Franciscan poverty' to mark a certain distinctive emphasis in the practice of abnegation, so it is possible to speak of 'Marian' charity to indicate a special way of practising charity.

As soon as union with Mary has taken root in a soul, it develops a deeper, stronger and more personal love for men than ever it knew before, thus communicating to the Legionary refinements of tenderness, or, as the Manual puts it, 'sweet reverence.'

The glory of charity, it has been said, is to be able to foresee. It is characteristic of mothers that they can divine unacknowledged troubles. 'Marian' charity enjoys this privilege. It does not treat men *en masse* or as if they were mass-produced. It approaches them rather one by one, knowing that each has his own problem, and that in the secret recesses of his mind nothing is so unlike one man as another. Men willingly wear masks: they like drawing red herrings across the path and confusing the scent. They refuse to be overcome by force, and their self-respect jibs at overmastering logic. 'Every time I win an argument,' said a well-known apologist, 'I lose a soul.' And a preacher once attributed all his success to the following rule: 'In every dispute,' he said, 'I take good care not to provoke my opponent, for as long as he remains unruffled, the grace of God, within him, is working on my side.'

What selflessness and tact that requires! It will be perceived to what degree, union with Mary will transform contacts made in the apostolate, and will give the power to persuade without offending, retiring gentleness and a wholesome respect for others which is really an extension of the reverence of God Himself. *Cum magna reverentia disposuit nos*, St. Augustine said of God. He treats us with great respect. But apostolic respect is not the fashionable form of respect for others which means leaving everyone to go to perdition in his own way on the ground that he knows his own business best. As if being a Christian did not imply responsibility for the salvation of our brothers, and forfeiture of the right to stand aside. 'Cain, where is thy brother Abel?' Does not God put this question to each of us at the present day? The liberal world finds such slogans as *Laisser faire* and every man for himself, very convenient, but they are the antithesis of Catholicism. Of course we must choose with wisdom—natural and supernatural—the right moment, the means, and the suitable note to strike. But we have no right to take refuge in silence. It is a delicate problem which union with Mary makes it ever easier to solve. She associates us with her motherhood, ever on the watch, with her love which can never offend for it is shot through and through with another Love.

To simple and even uncouth souls, she gives the means for refinements of perception. A supernatural nobility of soul, an exquisite courtesy, is a certain indication of union with God, a sure sign of His presence.

Union with Mary is the short, straight way, giving to those souls, responsive to her promptings, the necessary skill and tact. Think how Our Lady spoke to Bernadette at the Apparition on February 18: 'Will you be good enough to come every day for a fortnight?' That was how the Queen of Heaven addressed an ignorant child. It can be said that Mary never treats anyone as a superior speaking to an inferior, nor even as an equal addressing her peers. Always she speaks as an inferior to a superior because she sees Jesus Christ in every soul that comes to her and because for ever her only attitude is that of the Servant of the Lord.

The Marian apostolate can invariably be recognized by that tone and that respect. May the Legionary hear it said of himself, as it was of St. Peter: 'Thy speech doth discover thee.'

Union with Mary and Personal Sanctification.

Nor is this all, for the soul of the Legionary also undergoes a gradual change. Canon Guynot, who had seen it happen, describes it as follows:

'Until then his charity had been that of Christians of the world. He spoke of his neighbours freely enough; he spoke of what he knew, without scruple, on the ground that the facts were known, or soon would be, or were of small moment; with equal freedom he expressed his criticisms, his astonishment and sometimes his indignation, he allowed himself without the least remorse to reveal the failings and blunders of his neighbours. On the other hand he thought it quite permissible to react vigorously against anything that vexed him or upset his plans. He thought he could make an interior judgment of all that he considered blameworthy in what he saw around him, and he persuaded himself, that it was enough to keep these judgments to himself, or to mention them only within his own small circle, to be free of all reproach. Tell me, do you think this picture too black. . . ?

'What is quite certain is that this way of thinking and acting cannot last long in a true Legionary. For the true Legionary, who is docilely formed by the Legion, is not slow to acquire the feeling of a mother's heart, the heart of Mary, towards all men, and a mother has such sensitive charity, such refinements of tenderness, such consideration as will be always unsuspected in any save herself.

'Mothers take trouble to cover up the faults of their children: I must hide the faults of my brother, or, if I must reveal them I keep his name dark, or, if I really cannot escape the duty of making them known, I mention only those which must be reported, never more, just as a surgeon cuts into the flesh only where it is vital, and makes no wound larger or deeper than is absolutely necessary. . . .' [30]

What is the secret of such 'maternal' charity? Union with Mary.

This fusion of soul progressively engenders the refinement we have just described. In union with the most blessed Virgin, the Legionary knows, by instinct, how unkind, sarcastic or biting words are out of tune with the gentleness of Mary. His union with her leads him to see his neighbours with new eyes, Mary's eyes, to speak of them with a new tongue, Mary's tongue, to love him with a new heart, Mary's heart.

This metamorphosis takes place gradually and imbues his life with the 'perfume of Christ' which is the joy of the Church. Imparting to 'her soldier and her child' her own tastes, her intimate feelings and the marvels of her ingenuity, Mary establishes her reign in the heart of the Legionary. He thinks only of others, but his mother appreciates his self-sacrifice and ennobles his soul, thus once more demonstrating that he who loses his soul shall save it.

Whether as a school of the apostolate or a school of personal sanctification, it makes no difference: Mary, 'kindest and most generous of creatures' does not allow herself to be outdone in generosity. If when the Legionary turns harrassed from some 'fruitless' errand of the apostolate, he could only see in the mirror of his own soul the spiritual fruit of this failure, as of all his efforts, he would fall upon his knees to give thanks to God for having, all unbeknown, accomplished such great things in him.

CHAPTER V.

APOSTOLIC COURAGE

SO, TAKING IN MY HAND THE LEGIONARY STANDARD, WHICH SEEKS TO SET BEFORE OUR EYES THESE THINGS, I STAND BEFORE THEE AS HER SOLDIER AND CHILD, AND I SO DECLARE MY ENTIRE DEPENDENCE ON HER. SHE IS THE MOTHER OF MY SOUL. HER HEART AND MINE ARE ONE.

WE ARE unused to coupling the two words 'soldier' and 'child' together. 'Child' suggests dependence, passivity, receptiveness. 'Soldier' suggests initiative, vigour, a fighting spirit. We are nothing, *servi inutiles sumus*, less than a child. But we are also fellow-workers with God.

Pause for a moment to consider what is here required of us.

'Child.' I declare my entire dependance. Mary is the mother of my soul: her heart and mine are as one.

These words are full of meaning, and we have only hinted at the riches that they hide. They call on us to give ourselves up to God—in Mary—in complete abandonment, to acknowledge His absolute supremacy: God alone is God, and it is He who attains all things from first to last. His grace is sovereign. His word is a keen sword. He disposes of men and moments as it pleases Him. On the road to Damascus He struck down Saul, transforming him thereby into the Apostle of the Gentiles. His grace is free as He is and the Spirit bloweth where it listeth. He refuses to let Himself be confined by us and, if it seems good to him, ignores our schemes and the limits we contrive. *Cogitationes meae non sunt cogitationes vestrae*: 'My thoughts are not your thoughts and my ways are not your ways.' It is important to know this from our own experience lest the apostolate should become our private affair. God leads and only God knows the way. God wishes to find in us docile, tractable souls through whom He can work. That is the immutable truth. It behoves us never to forget it in practice.

And yet the sovereign, all-powerful God who created the world with a simple 'fiat' has willed to stand in need of our help. God offers and requires our collaboration with Him. He invites us, the useless servants, to be partners with Him: *Dei adjutores*.

Moreover He will not accept from us lip service only, or a mere hand's turn. Lip service is content with a few hasty prayers. The world is bad, it is said, so bad as to be incapable of transformation. There is nothing we can do; only pray for the unhappy souls who are being lost. 'Let us pray' is often an escape or an alibi. Excellent if it results in solid prayer, but the 'let us pray' is all too frequently a pious hope backed by little reality. Needless to say here, we are not referring to a contemplative life of immeasurable value, which is a special, exceptional vocation. For the Christian living in the world, real prayer is that which goes before action, and is its necessary concomitant. Human action is for God what water is in baptism, and bread in the Eucharist: the material for divine operation. We cannot do without prayer, but it must be prolonged in action. I ought to plead to God for my neighbour in danger, but I should also hold out a hand to save him from drowning. The same Master who told us to 'pray without ceasing' commanded us also to go out and act.

'The things I pray for, dear Lord,' prayed Saint Thomas More, 'give me grace to labour for.' ([31])

The Legion intends to respect and practise this duty of co-operation which is requisite for the work of God. It embodies its concept in military language in order to emphasise its longing to serve God with courage worthy of Him.

1. *Courage, a Necessary Virtue.*

The dominant word in this paragraph is SOLDIER and the action which it emphasizes is the holding of the standard. This

Vexillum was chosen purposely in imitation of the Roman Legionary standard and its name has been borrowed from theirs.

The reason for this choice is that, historically, the Roman Legion stands for what was a picked body of legendary courage and loyalty. It was the Roman Legionaries who held the outposts of empire and who faced the constantly recurring invasions. The Manual quotes not without ulterior motive, the example of that Roman centurion who was found at his post beneath the ruins and lava of Pompeii, and recalls the memory of the Theban Legion massacred for its faith during the persecution under Maximinus. It reminds us, too, of the Legionary who saw Christ die and who —the first of millions—glorified the Most High, crying 'Indeed this was the Son of God.'

This homage offered to Roman gallantry inspires us to imitation. Forcibly it emphasizes that courage is an indispensable virtue in the service of God, and a special characteristic of genuine Marian devotion. Remember what Bl. Pius X said: 'The greatest obstacle to the apostolate is the timidity, or rather the cowardice, of the faithful.'

The Legion is determined not to deserve this reproach, which all too often is true. Consequently it requires of its members moral courage as an integral part of their duty as Christians. Heroism is no optional luxury, something extra to duty, as we would sometimes like to lead people to believe. Not always, at least. The doctor treating an infectious case is only doing his professional duty, and the soldier who, at the risk of his life, obeys the command to attack is only carrying out his bounden duty. Why not dare to take the same view of apostolic duty? How singularly cautious and fearful we are about God's affairs. Instinctively we become casuists. This is one of the strongest reasons why too many Catholics do not lead unbelievers, as Rivière put it, into the 'temptation to believe.' Yet courage is a virtue which exercises great attraction and is more effective than the most eloquent discourse in the world.

The Legion, in requiring its members to make their apostolic visits in pairs, is aware that it requires a difficult service. He who would face a barrage of shells without flinching, finds himself weakening before the ridicule or the mocking smile lying in wait behind a strange door. Severe penances on bread and water are less difficult than this risk of the apostolate, and more than one Legionary would unhesitatingly prefer a day of absolute silence to this venture into the darkness in search of lost sheep. Nothing is more paralysing than this subtle fear which is called 'human respect.' It made St. Peter tremble before the servant of the high Priest. Yet once human respect gets the upper hand, all work for souls is at once reduced to insignificant proportions. The fear of a direct approach in the apostolate often leads men to relegate it to the background. Pope Pius XII puts us on our guard against this reversal of values: 'Who is not sad at heart.' he asks, 'to see how economic misery and social ills increase the difficulties of Christian life. . .? But that does not allow us to infer that the Church should begin by putting aside her mission and obtain first the alleviation of social ills. Although the Church sets herself always to defend and promote justice, since the Apostles, she has carried out the mission for the sanctification of souls . . . seeking the while to fight against social evils, for she knows that religious influences and Christian principles are their best cure.' (May 3, 1951).

If the Apostles had waited until all social and political injustices were put right before they preached the Gospel, the world would not yet have received their message. We must, therefore, forge ahead without delay, fearing neither failure nor suffering. Souls must be paid for. A Spanish proverb attributes these words to God 'Take, what you will, but pay the price.' God loves a brave soul.

That is why the Legion has chosen a military name, and expects those who rally to it to think of themselves as soldiers on active service. It has made apostolic courage its distinctive mark by which it would like to be known. But it regards this courage, also, as a Marian virtue.

2. *Courage, a Marian Virtue.*

We are hardly used to seeing Our Lady as the absolute embodiment of human courage. Her maternal gentleness partly hides from us her virile virtues. Still, she is Queen of the Apostles, of doctors, of martyrs, that is, of the pioneers who blazed the Gospel trail, who fought for its teachings and died for it. Like St. Theresa, of Lisieux, but a thousand times more, she experiences in her soul each of these calls to heroism; she, who stood by each of these heroes in the struggle. Warrior Virgin she is *par excellence* for she leads the attack on Satan.

'I will put enmities between thee and the woman, and thy seed and her seed: she shall crush thy head and thou shalt lie in wait for her heel.' (*Genesis* 3, 15).

In this woman of Genesis, arrayed against the serpent, the Church sees Mary. To her, Mary appears as she who brings God's battles to victory, whose name is terrible as an army ranged for battle. We must, therefore, study more closely this incomparable valiancy of soul.

Our Lady's courage stands out clearly, from the very first known incident of her life. Mary made a vow of perpetual chastity. In her world and at her time, this was not a common practice. It needed rare courage to dare to make such a vow for it exposed her to the disapproval of all her circle, and ran counter to established custom. Mary did not hesitate to offer this sacrifice to God.

This first hint of her strength of soul was to be confirmed by her whole attitude at the Annunciation. What the angel proposed to her was beyond all human possibility. He offered her a virginal motherhood to be effected in her solely by the Spirit of God. The angel asked her consent without telling her how she was to be vindicated in the eyes of men. By saying 'yes' she plunged in anguish Joseph, whom she loved as no woman ever loved her betrothed before, for the human heart is not cramped by holiness, but heightened in its power to love. She staked her reputation and, according to the usage of her time, her very life. However glorious the invitation, only a soul of no ordinary stamp could have accepted the adventure of faith with all its consequences. As soon as she grasped the message she gave unhesitating acceptance: 'Be it done unto me according to Thy word.' It is the leap into the unknown, an absolute and unconditional surrender. *Deus providebit*, The Lord will provide.

Moreover, in agreeing to become the mother of Jesus, Mary knew that she entered wholly into a mystery of Redemption. She knew the Scriptures and had read in the pages of Isaia about the Man of Sorrows. She knew—before the prophecy of Simeon, and doubtless with a clarity that increased daily—that she would be linked as no other creature could be with the Passion of her Son. Her acceptance was not merely a general consent to God's will, but, though veiled by her humility, specifically a heroic choice.

When Simeon spoke to her of the sword which should pierce her heart, she heard the prophecy without weakening and like a treasure hid it away among those things which she kept and 'pondered in her heart.' Her only concern was of fidelity to her task. She asked neither the why nor the wherefore. Sorrow found her always ready; her soul, from the very first, was prepared. There was no thought of self: God's glory and His dear will alone mattered. The Gospel records as a matter of course, that Mary stood at the foot of the Cross on Calvary. She was there in the thick of the mob, whereas the apostles had fled, for she had to unite her compassion with the redemptive Passion. Her faith penetrated every veil, every outrage, every wound; her whole soul was united, trembling yet clear-sighted, with the mystery of salvation enacted before her. Her part therein, was to give mankind's consent and she did not refuse it. The Church has condemned those who dared to speak of Mary's collapsing and disapproves those artists who depict her so. For Mary is the 'strong woman' above all others, though more sensitive, more vulnerable to hurt than all the rest, but braver than all the martyrs whose Queen she is.

Turris eburnea, Ivory Tower: thus we call her, for strength of soul is an inseparable characteristic of the Immaculate Virgin at each turning point of her life. Never was anyone more courageous than this woman. Except Christ Himself, the world has never known such delicacy of soul allied with such self-mastering courage.

It is not without reason, then, that the Manual calls on the Legionary to draw inspiration from his Queen that he may learn an important lesson of fortitude.

'The spirit of the Legion is that of Mary herself,' it says. Especially does the Legion aspire after . . . her self-sacrificing courageous love of God. . . . Her Legion essays any and every work, and 'complains not of impossibility, because it conceives that it may and can do all things.' And that is not mere bravado.

3. *Courage in the Face of the Impossible.*

Union with Mary confers on her soldiers a special kind of courage in face of the impossible. It is a tenet dear to the Legion that the impossible is possible. Or more precisely, in picturesque terms, 'The impossible sub-divides into a given number of situations, each of which is possible.' A paradox, if you will, but a paradox proved by experience. What does it mean? It means that we must never take refuge behind the word 'impossible' in order to refuse an apostolic labour. It means that the surest way of bringing an 'impossible' enterprise to a successful conclusion is to take the first—and possible—step in the right direction. I cannot at once reach the summit of a mountain, but it is always possible to climb first one height and then another, and so on right to the top. Every possibility achieved, opens the way to a new possibility. It is the triumph of *divide et impera*, divide and rule. Is that a truism? Maybe, but if it goes without saying it 'goes' a great deal better if said. And better still if tried! None of the spiritual successes in Dublin were attempted without exclamations of 'Impossible' on all sides. Clean up Bentley Place, century-old haunt of every vice; give retreats to prostitutes; start days of recollection for Protestants; change the tramps of the Morning Star into apostles; all this was labelled folly. All these and how many other missions undertaken there and elsewhere, were labelled crazy? For such imagined impossibilities the treatment is the same as for Alpine peaks: from the distance they appear insurmountable. Then one day a bold mountaineer scales the first peak, then the second, the third and finally ... the last. It is not necessary when the first step is taken to see clearly how the second is to be managed, still less the last. It is enough to believe that God has entrusted to us the first step and that if need be He will cope with the last stage.

We have a natural tendency to qualify a given task as impossible and a given case as hopeless. Yet what do we know about it? The goodness of God upsets our calculations, confounds our terrors.

The conquering hand of Christ reaches out to the most rebellious souls, and the story of the lightning on the road to Damascus is constantly re-enacted. There is no end to instances of the intervention of God's mercy. God is on the watch and His infinitely resourceful and tenacious love swoops down on the most hardened cases as does an eagle on its prey. So how am I to know if I have done enough for this soul? By what standard can God's patience be measured? Look closely and you will see that quite a number of 'impossibilities' have been proved quite possible. Besides, why eliminate from the Gospel 'with God all things are possible'? It is enough for us to try, knowing that step by step God will help us to pass through the portal of the impossible and so enter into the land promised to our faith.

Such courage is rare. It is nonetheless imperative. In this sphere Our Lord does not judge as we do. We are full of admiration for St. Peter walking upon the water to meet the Master. And

Jesus greets him with 'Why hast thou doubted, oh man of little faith?' We seldom accuse ourselves of weakness of faith, yet there precisely is a subject for examination of conscience which could disclose an unpleasant surprise for us. What progress Christians would make if they could only be ashamed of their wretchedly weak faith and say with their whole being, 'Lord, I believe, help thou mine unbelief.'

As a direct application of this principle, suppose we scrutinize our own attitude to the problem of bringing the masses back to God and the Church. Do we honestly believe that this return is possible, or is it not rather a dream or a slogan that we repeat without real assent? There is a sort of apostolic pessimism compounded of incredulity and distrust of God. There are comfortable doctrines which are widespread but the exact contrary to Our Lord's commands. There are forms of weariness more harmful than apostacy, for they form the atmosphere in which defeatism flourishes instead of shaking it off at once. Woe to him who robs his brother of the courage to believe the Gospel today, and to act on it wholeheartedly.

The Legion intends to immunize its members against such unconscious cowardice. It points to the neo-pagan masses peopling our cities and says that with a deliberate will to win them—if every Catholic had an apostolic soul—it would be 'possible,' after the first effort loyally exerted, to bring five per cent. of these masses back to Christianity.

And why should not this first assault lead to another, and then another and so on? To recoil before the magnitude of the enterprise is simply to ignore that division of the 'impossible' of which we spoke above.

Sometimes, of course, it must be admitted, we do not quite see how this first shock should be launched. So what is to be done? Anything, the Legion answers, so long as you do not remain inactive. If you can see no further, well then, rather than folding your arms, make a gesture, no matter how small, in the direction aimed at. This is called 'symbolic action.' Such was the offering of the boy in the Gospel who brought to the Master 'five loaves and two fishes.' How feed the multitude on such meagre rations? Symbolic action again, a gesture disproportionate to its great aim, yet a gesture for which God chose to wait before exerting His omnipotence. A magnificent act of faith which causes us to give God our 'mite,' thus, by our very penury, appealing for His help. It may be added that this act of faith is also an effective element in human psychology.

For in a most practical way symbolic action emphasizes the need for effort. If we do not bestir ourselves we shall never achieve anything. Even in the natural order we can overcome obstacles if we make a real effort of will. 'Where there's a will there's a way.' For it is a fact that the human mind, disliking useless action, becomes more and more ingenious and probably ends by finding a way out. Furthermore, if I allow myself to be dominated by the idea of impossibility like a mountaineer confronted by sheer cliff, nothing will result; I shall be beaten before I begin, for every defeat saps morale and postpones victory. On the contrary, if, in spite of all, I act, I keep my soul prepared for the struggle, ready to seize the smallest chance of success.

When, during the American Civil War, Admiral Du Pont explained to Admiral Farragut why he had failed to take Charleston with his battle fleet, Farragut heard him to the end.

'There was another reason, Du Pont,' he answered.

'Was there? What?'

'You did not *believe* you could do it.'

That is a story with a moral for all times.

'To capitulate,' said Péguy, 'is essentially to explain instead of acting. And cowards are people bursting with explanations.'

Effort, even if it appears ineffectual, helps us to believe with a firm faith: it has, likewise, its function in the supernatural order. In union with Mary, who was the first to believe in the impossible, it leads, more often than we think, to success beyond our hopes.

In this school of confidence, little by little, the boundaries of the impossible shrink and fade away like night fades at the coming of dawn.

Hard tasks, however, will constantly appear and these the Legion prefers to the easier ones. By choice and instinct, the Legion makes for the difficult mission, and the thankless task which no one wants. 'There is no depth too low for the Legion to go in its search for lost sheep' says the Manual; and in answer to all apprehension, justified or not, it replies that it is very necessary that someone should assume these duties, and that there is no valour worth the name which does not, in some measure, recall the Colosseum.

'The Colosseum.' This word may sound unreal in these calculating days. 'But the Colosseum was a calculation, too,' says the Manual: The calculation of many lovely people—no more strong, no more weak than Legionaries of Mary—who said to themselves: 'What price shall a man give for a soul?'

These quotations, and others like them, bear their full significance for those who know the living history of the Legion. The sole example of Edel Quinn, who, when already gravely ill, left for Africa to take the Legion to the missionaries and died there, in Nairobi, in the heart of Kenya, after eight years of superhuman effort, should suffice to prove that these words of the Manual find an echo in souls today.

4. *Courage and latent Heroism.*

Heroism, thank God, is no inaccessible ideal. Under our very eyes examples are not lacking of Christians who love God to the very end. The Legion desires to increase their number and, in its own sphere, show that ideal in action.

More instances of heroism are to be found in the world than some suspect. Miners are trapped by an explosion, a group of mountaineers is caught by an avalanche, an aeroplane crashes in the desert, a ship runs aground: instantly heaven and earth are moved and numerous rescuers arrive on the spot; a comrade in danger is not left to his fate. The team sets off, haunted by the thought of tortured bodies and hopeless cries in the dark. They go because they have human hearts and cannot stand idle while such catastrophes occur. And it is very wonderful. Such scenes restore belief in man. But do we think of souls in peril? For them the Legion longs to organize and multiply rescue teams. 'What does it profit a man if he gain the whole world and lose his own soul?' The words are familiar, we try to estimate their meaning; in reality they are the measure of all else; they call for a school of supernatural heroism.

There are times when the heroism latent in men is suddenly aroused. For example, where the alarm is given and war breaks out, man stops judging things by conventional standards. He sees suddenly all that is at stake and things slip into their true proportion. And not seldom the complacent middle-class man, the Civil Servant fond of his comforts, turns out to be a brave man in time of danger. All little pretences collapse, words sound hollow, yesterday's pre-occupations today seem both childish and unpleasant. In danger the soul opens out, for good and sometimes, unfortunately, for evil. In any case, peril reveals new men.

Now, a 'cold war' is engaged in the invisible world of souls. Daily we witness spiritual disasters, spiritual shipwreck. What are we waiting for? The suitable moment? But there are many such. We are waiting to be asked, then? But silent griefs are far more moving than the shrillest cries. Do we expect the man lying wounded by the roadside to recover consciousness and call out before we stoop to bind up his wounds? Do you know the indictment of a recently converted Austrian socialist, published in the form of a letter, 'Offener Brief eines Jungen Sozialisten' (Open Letter of a Young Socialist)? Here is the gist of it. 'I encountered Christ when I was twenty-eight. I think of the years before that meeting as lost years. But am I alone to blame for that loss?

APOSTOLIC COURAGE

Listen: no-one ever asked me to take an interest in Christianity.

'I had friends and acquaintances, practising Christians, fully aware of what religion brings to human life. . . . *But not one of them ever talked to me about his faith.*

'This though they knew I was neither an adventurer, nor immoral, nor yet a scoffer whose sarcasm was to be feared. I was simply one of thousands, one of those millions of young men who are neither good nor bad, with a very vague and erroneous impression of Christianity. . . .

'Do you know why I had to wait so long before I found out the truth?

'Because most believers are too indifferent, too fond of their comforts, too lazy. They do not bother themselves about their neighbours. . . .'

May God forgive us our sins of omission, our tranquil cowardice, the crime of inadequate love! With a world hungry and thirsty for God—that unknown God for whom man is groping—this is no time for the practice of routine religion, a Christian life centred upon self; every Catholic should cry his message from the roof-tops. In this connection Mgr. Ancel's words are relevant: 'It is said: "we can't talk to them of Christ . . . they are not ready." That may be true . . . but more often it is we who are not ready.'

In our world of today, more than ever, the need is for a strong, courageous Catholicism, heedful of the tremendous spiritual distress which surrounds us. And so the Legion expresses its Marian devotion in military terms. The Vexillum is heir to the standard of the Roman Legion to remind us of that manly virtue of courage. By grasping it as he makes his Promise the Legionary forms an alliance between himself and Mary, the Queen of God's battles.

'*I stand before Thee as her soldier and her child.*' These words appeal to a love that does not falter, and will remain faithful until death.

CHAPTER VI.

HUMANITY AND APOSTOLIC STRENGTH

AND FROM THAT SINGLE HEART SHE SPEAKS AGAIN THOSE WORDS OF OLD: 'BEHOLD THE HANDMAID OF THE LORD.' AND ONCE AGAIN THOU COMEST BY HER TO DO GREAT THINGS. LET THY POWER OVERSHADOW ME, AND COME, INTO MY SOUL WITH FIRE AND LOVE, AND MAKE IT ONE WITH MARY'S LOVE AND MARY'S WILL TO SAVE THE WORLD.

1. *The Humility of Our Lady.*

'Behold the handmaid of the Lord.'

All Mary's soul is in these words; thus her humility remains inviolate even though she went forward to meet the divine advance and an unparalleled proposal.

Not one moment of self-glorification did she feel.

Not one glance of complacency did she bestow upon herself.

She offered her soul to God that the divine will might work on her and through her.

She is a pure transparency.

Mary is a mirror faithfully reflecting back to God every ray of His countenance.

She knows herself to be nothing in His sight.

She is only a creature: she depends entirely upon God who unceasingly draws her from nothing, and it is her joy to acknowledge it by sinking ever deeper into her humility. Her wealth is derived from a larger share of the Creator's liberality. She is, indeed, more a creature than any other. That is the avowal which springs from her soul; that is the cry of her heart which subjects her to the Holy Spirit.

Respexit humilitatem ancillae suae, thus she sang a few days later in her Magnificat. God hath regarded the lowliness of His handmaid; He deigned to choose the creature who, on earth, was most conscious of her own nothingness before Him.

Mary is the greatest depth offered to the sight of the God of Heaven, and that is why He pours Himself into her in torrents. She consented to her nothingness. Empty of herself, she could be flooded, like a brimming vase, with the fullness of God. *Ave gratia plena*.

She could not be proud. She feels her total dependence, her continuous state of receptivity, the unqualified gratuitousness of that love which embraced and filled her.

With certain intensities of grace, pride is incompatible. In the life of Bl. Angela de Foligno, it is recorded that the Holy Ghost said to her one day:

'I will do great things in you, which will be seen of all the world, in you I shall be known, glorified, and surrounded with brightness.'

The saint, upset at these words, exclaimed:

'If you were really the Holy Ghost you would not address me with words so unsuitable for me, or so dangerous, for I am frail, and they might well make me proud.'

'Very well,' said He, 'Try if you like. See if you can be proud....'

'Then,' Bl. Angela goes on, 'I made great efforts to feel proud to see if the voice had told me the truth.... But all my sins came back to mind; I could see only faults and vices in myself; and I felt in my soul a humility such as I had never known before.'

This glimpse into the soul of Angela de Foligno, gives us an inkling of what happened in that of Mary. What was a passing grace in the saint, is the very texture of Our Lady's soul, her breath, her way of realizing that God is all and that she is as nothing before Him. It is not the memory of sin, but the vivid experience of her own nothingness, that steeps the stainless one in this matchless humility.

2. *Legionary Humility.*

The Legion which boasts her name should make it a duty to be associated with this particularly Marian virtue.

'If union with Mary,' it says, 'is the indispensable condition, the root, so to speak, of all activity, the soil it needs to grow in, is none other than humility. If the soil is poor the life of the Legionary can but languish and perish.' (Manual).

We must, therefore, resolutely enter into the humility of Mary, if we would offer ourselves to the Holy Ghost that He may work through us, if we are to be tractable souls for God, to use in His mighty schemes. Humility alone can blaze the trail for God to come and perform His mysterious works, for He does not will that His work should suffer interference or be deflected by the distortions of our self-love. He wills to follow His path unhindered and show forth His strength and power without the instrument that He has chosen, compromising His work for a single instant. He will have no equivocation, it is He and He alone who gives Himself through us. As soon as His tool loses its suppleness with some hidden self-satisfaction or some unacknowledged self-seeking the flow ceases, the current is cut off. God is jealous of His unparalleled glory, not for Himself but because He loves us and knows we have need of Him alone: *Deus quaerit gloriam suam non propter se, sed propter nos*, St. Thomas was able to say. Nothing in us must be allowed to thwart His love, or hamper His infinite liberality. Not merely must we avoid putting the vanity of our self-sufficiency in His way, but we must humbly accept the fact that His ways are unexpected and disconcerting. We expected to meet Him at the cross-roads and He is with us on the way. He speaks and we fail to recognise His voice. He leaves us and we realize Who has gone, like the disciples at Emmaus. He joins Himself with us, yet all the time He is following His own course. If He leaves us it is the better to find us again. If He is silent it is to speak the more insistently. If He permits trials it is the closer to embrace us.

If He gives us pleasure it is the better to prepare us for tomorrow's cross.

Unpredictable, ever-astonishing God who constantly reminds us of His desire to be left a free hand, to use in His own way the tools which without Him are nothing.

Only by the royal road of humility can God be found. He can be given to others only by those who efface themselves before Him. Man closes up when confronted by another's pride; He opens like a flower in the sunshine when he feels himself in the presence of a soul stripped of self. For, in this emptiness, he can detect the fullness of the grace of God. This is a truth of vital importance to the Legionary who is called constantly to meet his brothers who do not know him.

If the Legionary can thus efface himself, he will allow God to show through, and virtue will go out from him. That which cannot be obtained by the most lucid arguments or the most well-meaning reproach, can often be extracted by a friendly brotherly word or two. That is why the Legion's method tends to give its proper place to this fundamental virtue.

In the Legionary's life there are two special occasions upon which the virtue of humility is put to the test—when he first joins the Legion and when he is formally enrolled among its ranks.

At the outset, the candidate is asked to accept, as simply as a child, all the requirements of the Legion. It is a common occurrence that such and such a point may offend or give rise to a difference of opinion. The Legion realises this and rejoices in it —not for the sake of the shock itself, but for the docility of soul to which it invites the candidate and prepares him. It is dangerous to come to the Legion with the outlook of a reformer, anxious to debate, point by point, every syllable of its rule. We are tired to death of people who have their own ideas of reform and the phrase 'the plague of initiative,' is well justified. The Legion asks of its members humility without reserve and unqualified compliance. Therein lies one of the secrets of its strength.

Once the choice has been made, once the candidate has entered the Legion willingly, he must learn to remain steadfast; and here again the Legion takes no risks. It imposes a very strict discipline upon its members. Apart altogether, for the moment, from the merits of obedience, this discipline is a source of constant humility. To accept the appointed task and to perform it conscientiously; to give an account of one's work in the presence of all the other members; to go back to the ranks, when the time comes, after three or six years in office—all this is not gratifying to self-love. But it is a valuable lesson in self-effacement.

Nor is this all. Personal humility is certainly essential, but Legionaries must also practise a much neglected form of self-sacrifice—what may be called corporate humility. Pius XII, addressing the members of Italian Catholic Action, on September 7, 1947, made an urgent appeal for this type of unselfishness. He said, 'Wherever you meet sincere goodwill, activity, intelligence, shrewdness, directed towards the cause of Christ and His Church, whether in your own ranks or outside Catholic Action, even if these qualities are present under new, but sound, forms of the apostolate, rejoice in them. Do not hinder them; on the contrary, maintain a true friendship with them and help them whenever your support is feasible, desired or expected. So many and such pressing needs beset the Church today, that we must welcome every hand which offers generous co-operation.'

It is possible to be humble in ourselves but to show no sign of humility in regard to the group to which we belong. Unfortunately this is no rare thing. This failing is at the origin of many manifestations of totalitarianism, unrecognised for what they are, and different varieties of spiritual domination.

The Legion desires, as a body, to be humbly at the service of all. It refuses to be an isolated organization beside other organizations; it desires to be an organization at the service of all the works of God. It wants to serve other works as Mary served her cousin Elizabeth, with no other thought than to give a helping hand wherever needed—silently, modestly, without looking for thanks, as a matter of course. This love of self-effacement will make it turn, for preference, towards the poor and the unhappy, towards the lost and hopeless cases, towards the humdrum task and the difficult mission. This preference forms, in itself, an integral part of Legionary devotion to Mary.

All this the words of the Promise declare: *And from that single heart she speaks again those words of old*: 'Behold the handmaid of the Lord.'

3. Daring, a Virtue of the Humble.

'And Once Again Thou Comest by Her to do Great Things.'

Humility gives place, without transition, to tranquil daring. The Legion, once it has acknowledged and admitted the weakness of the instrument, like St. Paul, knows that this weakness is its strength, that God's creative work starts from nothing.

Its initial humility by acceptance of 'without Me, ye are nothing worth,' has its complement in that final daring founded on this other certainty, 'With Me, you can do all things.'

That is why, having repeated with Mary her *'Behold the handmaid of the Lord,'* the Promise adds: *And once again Thou comest by her to do great things.*

May the power of the Holy Ghost overshadow and enter into our souls, bringing His fire and love, and at once great things, worthy of God's love for the world, will appear.

Only the humble are truly bold. Expecting nothing of themselves, they know that they can expect everything of God. These great things which the Legion expects of the Holy Ghost, working once again today through Mary, are neither more nor less than the return of the pagan or de-christianized masses to God.

It hopes for that return of the masses to the fold, dreamt of by Leo XIII, followed up untiringly by his successors as the highest aim of the apostolate.

Misereor super turbam. 'I have compassion on the multitude,' said Our Lord. When this crowd, which had followed Him into the desert had nothing to eat, the disciples asked the Master to send it away to the neighbouring villages to buy food, but that was not Christ's intention. 'Give you them to eat,' He ordered.

The stupefied apostles protested, counting heads . . . till, looking about they found a boy who had five barley loaves and two small fishes. As a gift this was quite out of proportion to the need, a ridiculous offering, but one which Jesus accepted and blessed for the sustenance of the crowd.

The Legion, too, is obsessed with crowds. It knows that it cannot send them away empty-handed to seek nourishment from false prophets and that souls will find no food in those 'neighbouring villages,' which signify, so far as the intelligence and the heart are concerned, our pseudo-mystical contemporaries.

The Legion has heard Our Lord's insistent command:

'Give *you* them to eat.'

And the Legion offers itself—without protesting or weighing the difficulties—like the boy with the loaves and fishes; that is, it offers its prayers, its weekly proceedings, its discipline and its unreasoning confidence. It is enough for Jesus to envelop these poor human things with His divine blessing. And already the baskets begin to heap up.

The secret of the apostolate to the masses is one very simple conviction: the Legion believes that a crowd is made up of individuals; that a million men is in its totality one million personal souls, a million worlds, which must be approached one by one as the apostles offered the miraculous bread to those outstretched hands. One by one, with no fevered haste, they should be approached, because each immortal soul is worth more than the whole material universe, and reverence and reserve are required in contact with each one of them, like entering a church. One by one they should be approached because each soul is a personal problem, and has cost all the redeeming Blood of Our Lord. We say *all* the Blood, not just a drop, despite Pascal's moving words, 'I poured out this drop of My Blood for thee.' That is not enough. God so loved each soul that He paid the whole price of Redemption for him, as though he were alone in the world. *Dilexit me et tradidit semetipsum pro me.* 'He loved me and delivered Himself for me.' (*Gal.* 2, 20).

The Legionary, then, realizes that he must approach a soul with the uttermost respect: *Hic locus sanctus est.* 'This is holy ground.' The more he does so—in and through Mary—the more will he treat the soul as a living, sacred pyx, as a presence of God. But he is obsessed with the idea of the multitude, he thinks of it all the time as he speaks into the ears and looks into the eyes there before him.

If the masses are to be reached some institutional methods must, of course, be employed. There are indispensable techniques to create a milieu or to cure its ills, to purify the air, to drain the Pontine marshes. When an epidemic breaks out general methods of prevention and cure must be used; but the evil will be cured only if the doctors, sometimes even at the risk of their own lives, agree to treat each infected case individually.

Then, too, it is essential and a matter of urgency to make use of all methods of forming public opinion: the press, the radio, the cinema must be employed to influence the masses who are left quite defenceless against the frequently evil hold exerted by them. The Legionary co-operates willingly in this work of public welfare; but he believes, too, that in going from door to door, from soul to soul he fulfils an indispensable and beneficial mission. He knows that the task is too great for him, but humility develops an unlimited confidence in him. He dares to ask: '*make my soul one with Mary's love and Mary's will to save the world.*'

It is, then, in Mary's own way that he approaches souls: seeing the whole world yet yearning over each man as though there were only he. His attitude is like that of a mother who feeds a whole family, not as one unit, but child by child, who loves each one with a love personal to him yet common to the family, to whom the puny or sickly child is the favourite yet who is all to all. This is a miracle of single and collective love, a giving of self always different yet always the same. For is not maternal love, here on earth, by the depth of its individual application as in its inclusiveness which multiplies it without decreasing the gift of self, the closest image of the love of God?

4. *Audacity and the Conversion of the Masses.*

Misereor Super Turbam.

Today, more than ever, the world needs that cry of compassion. We have allowed men to become 'the masses,' and the human person to be submerged in the crowd like a drop of water in the ocean. The crowd screens the individual from us and prevents access to him. These are the crowds we rub shoulders with at factory gates, the crowds queueing for shows, the nameless, faceless crowds whom we jostle in the streets.

These millions, despite a certain level of secular culture, know less than a child about their eternal destiny or the religion of Christ. How are we to get into touch with them? As no one among these men has a soul to spare, it is now at once that they must be saved. Their intimate consciousness cannot be reached by mass production methods. Crowds can be roused by techniques of propaganda but they cannot make a man look into his own heart or surrender his soul.

For its own part, the Legion desires to transform these amorphous masses into individuals, so as to be able to establish with each one that indispensable personal contact which will set him free. Its apostolic technique aims at splitting up this ephemeral mass: hence those innumerable house to house visits, continued, if necessary, week after week throughout the year; hence, too, the more specialized activities such as book-barrows placed at selected points, and pickets posted in certain places where there is danger to faith or morals. The Legion strives to see the masses through the eyes of Mary, who knows each one of her children and calls them all by their own name. This is a gigantic, immeasurable task, but how well worthy of the servants of Our Lady!

Obviously, we cannot, of ourselves, reach every soul, nor bring to each one personally the message of Christ. Our days are only twenty-four hours long and our field of action is limited. Occasionally one hears: 'Give us saints and the world will be saved.' The truth is not quite so simple: the saints will save those souls whom Our Lord has attached to their souls. Those whom it is their mission to save. The individual is not personally responsible for the salvation of the human race, but he is for the salvation of the souls given into his care by the will of God. Their number varies. One single soul may thus be confided to me by God. Or perhaps God wills me to save ten thousand. Perhaps He has bound up the salvation of a million souls with the life of a Saint Theresa of Lisieux, cloistered in her convent. The number matters little, and the method of co-operation with the Redemption varies according to the differences of vocation, but each individual has his own particular part to fill, and if it is desired that the whole world should be saved, each Christian must be faithful to the care of the souls confided to him by God.

The Church does not recognize Christians without responsibility. Through me God longs to save such and such a soul: I cannot avoid it. He desires its salvation through my intervention, and is always eager to communicate Himself. Shall we never understand the words spoken by Our Lord to St. Angela of Foligno: 'I did not love you for fun'? It is not God's will that salvation should be delayed, and slowness is no law of providence. On the contrary, it is man's sin which hampers God's work: dilatoriness is born of our deficiencies. Throughout the Old Testament do we not see God complaining that the malice of men continually raises barriers in the way of His mercy? Without original sin our first parents would have transmitted supernatural life directly to all their descendants. By God's design they should have been born holy.

Sin thwarted this desire of God's, but it has not succeeded in doing away with His tenderness. Today, as in the beginning, God wills man's salvation. He desires earnestly with the impatience of love. But at the same time He desires that man should, as a rule, be saved by his brother, and that is why, if I were the only Christian in the world, I should have the grace of salvation for the whole human race because I should bear in myself all the saving love of God.

Faith in God's present, persevering, urgent, untiring love is the reason for the Legion's apostolic insistence and perseverance.

From this is derived also its appeal to all of good will to help in the task. The Legion envisages this mobilization of Catholic laity on a wide scale. Not from an itch for original methods, but because of the ordinary demands of normal Christianity. The duty of the apostolate, it says, echoing Popes, is not optional; it is obligatory. No one is baptized or confirmed for himself alone, and the destiny of our brothers is linked with our own. If, therefore, each member is asked to devote to it a few hours weekly, *ex professo*, there is implied only the clarification, the making explicit, of an already existing duty. That, in the Legion's view, is the minimum for those who are very busy. In fact, in this case, as elsewhere, those who have leisure hardly ever find any to devote themselves to others. Save for a few fortunate and rare exceptions, the Legion has in its ranks none but the unleisured.

This sense of an elementary, universal obligation to be fulfilled urges the Legion to welcome as a recruit every sincere Christian of goodwill. At the risk of repetition, we must reiterate that it is so easy to refuse this duty by pleading that the apostolate is the monopoly of saints and not the province of the ordinary laity. This cheap and questionable humility, sometimes encourages us to refuse our duty at the critical moment. It is a plausible pretext. Certainly the saints provide God with high-grade instruments, 'canals' through which redeeming grace can flow freely. But that does not alter the fact that the sinner is brother to the sinner next-door, and is responsible to a certain extent for his salvation. It is a favourite saying of the Legion's that the first Legionary in history was the good thief who, as he died, endeavoured to convert his fellow and received, so promptly, the reward: 'Today shalt thou be with Me in Paradise.'

Does not this awareness of the apostolate as a Catholic obligation spring from the purest tradition of the Church? For after all how did Christianity invade Europe? Was it not the merchant, the slave, the Roman Legionary who carried the good news, to his brother, speaking to him as man to man of the unknown God and of his great joy?

The very aims of the Legion oblige it to open wide its ranks to the volunteers for God's army to all those who agree to serve in union with Mary. The Legion opens its arms as wide as its Queen's and its prayers are infused with her limitless confidence:

'Let . . . my soul . . . be one with Mary's love and Mary's will to save the world.'

CHAPTER VII.

PURITY AND SPIRITUAL GROWTH

SO THAT I MAY BE PURE IN HER WHO WAS MADE IMMACULATE BY THEE; SO THAT CHRIST MY LORD MAY LIKEWISE GROW IN ME THROUGH THEE; SO THAT I WITH HER, HIS MOTHER, MAY BRING HIM TO THE WORLD AND TO THE SOULS WHO NEED HIM; SO THAT THEY AND I, THE BATTLE WON, MAY REIGN WITH HER FOR EVER IN THE GLORY OF THE BLESSED TRINITY.

THE LEGIONARY has opened his soul to the Holy Ghost to become an instrument in his apostolic work. For God's greater glory and the salvation of men, he has given himself up to God. So now let him for a moment look and see what he is and let him pray for himself.

1. *Apostolic Purity.*

Mary is and remains in God's sight, a creature and nothing. But we are sinful in addition. The disproportion between the work to be done and the instrument to carry it out, which we are, is glaring. The loftier the work entrusted to us, the purer our souls should be. The priest going up to the altar does not draw near to the holy of holies without first asking God to take away his 'iniquities' and to cleanse his lips as he did those of 'Isaias with a burning coal.' Every apostle about to be in contact with souls, feels his own unworthiness; for each soul, like a consecrated chalice, should not be handled by unclean hands. The livelier the apostle's faith, the better will he understand the need for purification before action. Like the priest we, too, must ask God: *Munda cor meum ac labia mea . . . ut digne valeam nuntiare evangelium tuum.* 'Cleanse my heart and my lips . . . that I may worthily announce thy holy Gospel.'

2. *Our Lady's Purity.*

Once again the answer to our anxiety and fears, lies in union with Mary.

'*That I may be pure in her who was made Immaculate by Thee.*'

What a magnificent mystery of grace is the union of the sinner with her who had the right to call herself the Immaculate Conception.

In Mary, there is not only an absence of sin, perfect subordination of body to soul and of soul to God, a crystalline purity. But between her and sin there is open warfare, an active incompatibility. It is she who, by virtue of her office, crushes Satan beneath her feet and untiringly defeats his works of darkness.

She is the light which puts the darkness to flight, the brightness which breaks up the shadows, and thwarts the most cunning of plots.

She is purity, ever making pure by the least breath of her mouth or the slightest touch of her hand.

She is everything that is purest and most beautiful: *Tota pulchra es Maria et macula non est in te*. Directly I unite myself to her, I feel myself at once called to live in union with her holy dispositions, with her exquisite delicacy of soul, with her revulsion from sin and her reaction against the slightest evil.

When we speak of impurity we generally think first of bodily impurity, that rebellion of the flesh against the spirit, which is in our nature since the Fall. Quite naturally, Mary is the refuge of tempted souls. Her very presence banishes danger, thought of her calms the imagination, her gentleness is a fresh breeze which stills temptation and drives away noxious airs. Never is 'pray for us sinners,' said to her in vain; at once she is bending over us, her arms stretched out.

She is also the refuge of the fallen. Devotion to Mary has proved the lifebelt and haven of salvation to many a soul, effecting sometimes an instantaneous and radical cure, a definite break with a past heavy on the conscience. For all she is the nearest remedy, easy to hand, the road to complete cure.

All this is the primary motive for saying:

'*That I may be pure in her who was made Immaculate by Thee.*'

But there is also a purity of soul that Mary will imperceptibly give us. The Apostle tells us not to 'quench the spirit' within us, and goes so far as to adjure us 'not to sadden it.'

By contact with Mary our moral conscience becomes refined. With heightened keenness we realize the horror of sin. *Iniquitatem odio habui*: dislike of evil is no longer enough for us, we shall learn to hate it. At Calvary the death of her Son affected Mary so profoundly that it can be said that it was a sort of death for her: *commori potuit*. Now, deicide is derived from sin itself, it is inherent in it. This was the sword that pierced her heart with sorrow.

How, then, could she fail to make us sharers in her feelings towards sin? How could her love fail to heighten in us delicacy of conscience, and the desire to flee from all contamination of evil? Our modern world has lost the sense of sin because it has lost the sense of God. For it the worst evil is an epidemic, famine or war; it understands with difficulty the unseen catastrophes and the crimes which cry only to Heaven for vengeance. Yet this physical evil which crushes the body is but a shadow of that other. A single venial sin, says St. Thomas, weighs heavier than all the ills of the world.

How, then, can mortal sin, with its incalculable damage and all the succession of its consequences, be qualified? One sin produces a series of others like a stone falling into water which ripples the whole surface with concentric circles. If we saw with the eyes of faith, and in its light, how greatly would our apostolic sense be endowed with a new keenness and breadth. A single sin avoided is a more valuable victory than the conquest of a continent. One soul torn from its chains and from the bondage of evil is a liberation celebrated in heaven by the nine choirs of angels. A sinner on his knees receiving absolution from his sins is an unfathomable mystery of God's mercy, and a unique joy thrilling the Father of the prodigal son and the maternal heart of Mary.

That I may be pure in her who was made Immaculate by Thee! So that I may detect and avoid anything which would be a refusal or savour of bargaining between myself and the Holy Ghost, anything that would soil myself or others. A soul is like a closed room whose sordidness is not at first sight apparent, but open the windows, let in the sunlight and how much unsuspected dust you will discover!

Allow Mary to enter a soul and open it to the Holy Spirit and at once a finer, more delicate standard of purity will be discerned and compel recognition. When at the altar we accuse ourselves of 'innumerable sins, offences and negligences,' we tend rather to think of them as a manner of speech, a conventional extravagance, but when we stand close to Mary Immaculate, we shall realize to the full, exactly what those words mean. Then we shall see these faults, like dust in the sunlight, we shall discover them in the very place we thought we were above reproach, in the corners where we seldom look. We shall see them in profusion in our judgments, conversations and deeds.

Union with Mary Immaculate will give to the Legionary the devotion to frequent confession, urged with such clear insistence by His Holiness Pope Pius XII in his encyclicals, *Mystici Corporis* and *Mediator Dei*. Our Lady of the Precious Blood will teach the Legionary to long for that purifying spring, which plunges him into the Blood of the Saviour. *Lavit nos a peccatis nostris in sanguino suo.* (Apoc. I. 5).

When Mary has given us light to see our sins and to hate them she will take us by the hand and lead us gently farther into that wide domain of our thoughts, not sinful, but useless. She will show us that every creature who approaches us, however holy he may seem, can be a danger for our soul, holding us back, a screen rising stealthily between God and us. She will show us how to avoid the fascination caused by the beauty of the things of this earth: she will deliver us from the subtle temptation of taking all our pleasure in them, at the risk of ceasing to refer all things to God as she does. She will have us say to all transient creation, the words Jesus used to Mary Magdalen in the garden, *noli me tangere*. Her uncompromising purity will permeate the innermost recesses of our souls to purify them. She will be for us that Shepherdess, sung by Alice Meynell, who guards her secret thoughts with jealous care:

> 'She holds her little thoughts in sight,
> Though gay they run and leap;
> She is so circumspect and right
> She has her soul to keep.' (32)

To keep one's soul for God is a task demanding constant vigilance. Mary is the ever faithful and most prudent virgin who never saddened the Holy Ghost; progressively she will give us that ever watchful correspondence with the Holy Spirit's inspirations that gladdens the heart of God.

Gradually we shall enter into her feelings, dispositions, intentions and operations. Since she is filled completely with, steeped in, the Holy Ghost, it follows, in consequence, that in her I inhale the Spirit, renouncing my own free will and my whole self to take on, or rather, to receive with docility, the designs of the Holy Spirit and thus become the instrument of His mighty purposes. Union with Mary leads by successive touches, unfailingly effective, to union with the Holy Ghost. It is not necessary to be aware of this; the mystery is accomplished in faith. 'The Holy Ghost shall come upon thee,' said the Archangel Gabriel, 'and the power of the Most High shall overshadow thee.' Under this same shadow these great things are effected.

We ask of Mary to receive the Holy Ghost through her because we know that her only ambition is to increase His influence on man and to prepare the way for His coming. There is no fear of illusion; we have at our command a sure sign by which to gauge and guarantee this work of Mary—the greater our union with her, the more pronounced in us does the mystery of purification become; the more we are emptied of self the more does God compel our recognition as the only God.

'How very true to life this is!' exclaims the Manual. 'The Legionary, in turning towards Mary, must necessarily turn away from self. Mary takes hold of this movement and elevates it; makes of it the supernatural dying to self which fulfils the stern but fruitful law of the Christian life. . . . The Legionary absorbed in love and admiration of his Queen is little inclined to turn from her to contemplate himself. . . . Completely submitted to Mary, the Legionary distrusts the promptings of his own inclinations and in all things, listens intently for the whisperings of grace. . . .'

What a school of purification is Mary! What a ceaseless death to self! What a conflict between her purity and our wretchedness. What a tower of David she is, watching over and protecting our weakness!

'Ah! how many cedars of Lebanon,' exclaims St. Louis de Montfort, 'how many stars of the firmament, have we not seen fall miserably, and lose in the twinkling of an eye all their splendour and brightness! What has brought about this strange reverse? It was not for want of grace, which is given to all, but it was for want of humility. They thought themselves capable of keeping their treasures; they trusted in themselves and relied on themselves. They thought their dwelling secure enough and their coffers strong enough to keep the precious treasure of their grace. It was because of that imperceptible self-reliance (although it seemed to them that they were relying solely on the grace of God) that the most just Lord allowed them to be robbed by leaving them to themselves.' (*True Devotion*, 88).

On the other hand, what sureness, what peace awaits those whose refuge and stronghold is Mary. Enveloped in her purity he dares, henceforward, to draw near to the throne of God. His wretchedness no longer makes him fearful for Mary has wrapped him about with her royal cloak.

> 'She causes him to be engulfed in the abyss of her graces;
> She adorns him with her merits;
> She supports him with her power;
> She illuminates him with her light;
> She inflames him with her love;
> She communicates to him her virtues, her humility, her faith, her purity;
> She makes herself his surety.'   (*True Devotion.* 144).

Mary makes up for us before God all that we lack. She is a creature like ourselves, and as Wordsworth said, 'our tainted nature's solitary boast.'

3. *Our Growth in Christ.*

The Promise goes on:

'So that Christ my Lord may likewise grow in me through Thee. . . .'
'So that I with her, His Mother, may bring Him to the world and to the souls who need Him.'

The constant labour of purification and renunciation has nothing negative about it, its purpose is wholly to encourage our continual growth in Jesus Christ. Born of divine charity it has no other aim but to increase it. Under the stimulus of the Holy Ghost we are transformed 'from glory to glory,' into the likeness of Our Lord, the One Model, for to Him, as we know, leads the action of the Holy Ghost through Mary.

What a delightful surprise will it be for the Legionary to discover one day, this slow working of grace effected in secret within him. Losing his soul for the sake of his brethren, he will find it, as the Gospel promises. This growth to full stature of Christ within him will be the immeasurable reward for his apostolic self-denial.

Experience teaches us that the surest way to nourish and preserve faith is to pass it on to others. Christianity cannot be safeguarded by building round it a Great Wall of China, even supposing that were possible today.

It is surprising how badly many Christians weather storms and that a mere change of surroundings will be enough to root out the whole practice of religion. So many of the lapsed of today, only yesterday were known as 'good Catholics.' Can they, in justice, be truly counted members of Christ? Can a Catholic confine himself to 'keeping the faith' like a treasure, buried in the ground? Did we receive it merely to 'keep it,' or to spread it abroad? What is the meaning of a Gospel which is not passed on as good tidings, of a message that is not sent, of a fire which will not burn, of a tongue which remains dumb? Yet that is the attitude of the 'good Catholic' who 'hides his light under a bushel.' What a caricature he gives of the religion he professes! In the early Church no sooner was Christ found than men ran to their brethren, as once Andrew did to Peter, to tell him: *Invenimus Messiam*: 'We have found the Messias.' And still today, is not this the natural reaction of the unbeliever, who has suddenly discovered the Faith? He cannot understand—and with reason—that such a treasure should be buried. His impulse is spontaneously to proclaim his discovery. That is a healthy reaction; it is we who are stale and settled down in our unpardonable routine ways. 'Catholics are really unbearable in their mystical security.' cried Péguy. 'But if they think the saints were inoffensive old gentlemen, they are much mistaken.'

And it is true. We have resigned ourselves to seeing the masses lapsing all around us. We have even worked out a convenient philosophy of non-interference. There are authors prepared to water down or twist the Gospel text which speaks of crying the truth from the roof-tops; these words appear to them as rather lacking in tact and, indeed, an intolerable intrusion on individual liberty of conscience. They even go so far as to say that in these days, when we are all so jealous of our independence and right to autonomy, the only convincing sermon is example, and that only of the most tactful kind. The very verb 'to proselytise' has become suspect as an unwarrantable interference and abuse.

We are told that the mission of the Church is not to convert the world, but to make Christian life possible and desirable to all men, and this under the specious pretext that the command to 'convert' mankind does not appear in Christ's missionary instructions. As forcefully as possible, it must be said that such theories are a flat contradiction of the truth. Our Lord based His teaching on the need for this radical change, the renewal of soul demanded by John the Precursor, and expressed by the one word 'repentance.' 'Repent and be converted.' Thus did the prophets inspired by God, thus did the apostles under the Master's direct orders. 'Going therefore, teach ye all nations: baptizing them in the name of the Father and of the Son and of the Holy Ghost.' Who would dare to assert that baptism does not imply a rebirth through penance and renunciation of Satan, as well as through total adherence to God? When St. Peter addressed the crowd which gathered after the healing of the lame man, he told them what he knew to be the commandment of the Lord: 'be converted.' When St. Paul spoke to the people of Lystra, who took him for a god, he protested, 'We also are mortals, men like unto you, preaching to you to be converted from these vain things to the living God.' Had these founders of the Church so entirely misconstructed the directions of the Master, and was it necessary to wait twenty centuries to discover that Christ meant to say that we should confine ourselves to discreet example? It is more than time to recover the value of words. *Vera vocabula rerum amisimus.* 'We have lost,' says Sallust, 'the real meaning of words.' By dint of speaking superficially of 'witness' and of 'presence,' the stage is reached of forgetting that in the New Testament, witnessing means primarily verbal proclamation of the Gospel. Jesus sends us forth to our contemporaries, as the Apostle was sent to the

Gentiles, 'To open their eyes, that they may be converted from darkness to light . . . that they may receive forgiveness of sins and a lot among the saints.' (*Acts* 26, 18).

It is no use pleading the duties and requirements of our state of life which monopolize the existence and activities of man in this world. As if the first duty of a Christian were not that which derives from baptism and makes him responsible for the salvation of his neighbour! And his neighbour means not merely his own family. Our age is marked by fear of responsibility. Which is tantamount to saying that it is profoundly 'dechristianized.' The baptized layman ought to understand that the apostolate is a normal, elementary duty, something which stands to reason and that the only permissible question is the precise form it will take. It is sometimes thought that the life of Our Lord is a model for the clergy alone, and not for every Christian; that is a fatal, pernicious error. Since Christ was to the highest degree an apostle, it follows that every Christian, a member of Christ, should also be one. The popes in reminding the laity of the urgent need for Catholic action have introduced no real novelty into the Church, nor propounded some unknown 'new organisation.' It is not an addition imposed suddenly on twentieth-century Catholics; it has been from the very beginning an imperative duty, the need for which compels more than ever urgent recognition. This renewal is being happily accomplished under our very eyes and the Christian layman is becoming increasingly aware of this essential duty. The Legion is not the only form it takes: *mansiones multae sunt in domo Domini*, but with all its power it desires to help this renewal of conscience and re-awakening.

Hence the Legionary asks the Holy Spirit:

So that Christ, my Lord, may likewise grow in me through Thee;
So that I with her, His mother, may bring Him to the world and
   to the souls who need Him.

To take Him to a world in distress, to a soul in peril, for there is no greater evil upon earth than not to receive the Saviour.

4. *Awaiting Christ.*

To give us courage a radiant vision is set before us: the final triumph of good over evil.

'*So that I and they, the battle won, may reign with her for ever in the Glory of the Blessed Trinity.*'

Time is short, the shape of this world is passing.

Caritas Christi urget nos. Christ's charity impels us to swift action for the day is at hand, the great and wonderful day when the Lord of glory will come to judge the living and the dead. This waiting for the coming of the Son of Man urges the Church to ceaseless pursuits of the work of evangelization.

Donec veniat. Until He come again: such is the order. Christians of the time of St. Peter lived this 'Advent' with all their strength convinced as they were of Our Lord's imminent return. They were mistaken about the date, but how they were buoyed up by this lively hope! But we no longer scan the horizon for signs of His coming. We should discover again that eager impatience. Who doesn't know Newman's wonderful sermon, *Waiting for Christ?*([33]) It should be read again to see vividly what a bracing effect such an expectation can give to our souls, and what wealth of heroic love lies hidden in it. One day we shall see Christ. He will come. We shall be like unto Him: *similes ei erimus.*

In this glory we shall find also the most glorious and blessed Virgin. Even now she is in heaven, glorified in soul and body. What a vision for the Legionary who is fighting for her! There she stands, his Queen, in the radiance of the Blessed Trinity, all flooded with the Holy Ghost who has completed His work in her. Her assumption is our pledge of hope and resurrection. Looking upon her we see in their perfection and unity the varied riches showered upon the Church throughout the ages. As Fr. L. Bouyer said, she is an image of the Church fulfilled at end of time.([34]) She, too, is waiting for us.

'Behold,' said St. Stephen to his executioners, 'I see the heavens opened and the Son of Man standing on the right hand of God.' (Acts, 7. 55).

We, too, should look into the opened heavens and in the glory of the Son contemplate that of His Mother; so will our pace be quickened, our indolence turned to vigour, our steps steadied, and our courage upheld. *Donec veniat!*

Time is short for the Church, but it is yet shorter for each one of us. We have only a few years to live and soon we shall have to give an account of the mission we have carried out. We shall have no right to claim that we have kept our talents in store and now return them intact. God will not accept this stewardship of His goods. We have to show the fruits of our Christian life and the souls we have led to Him. We have no time to lose; every hour, every minute is to be accounted for. 'Therefore,' wrote St. Paul to the Galatians, 'whilst we have time let us work good to all men.' (*Gal.* 6, 10).

The Legion longs to give to each soul this thirst, this obsession for the salvation of souls. It knows that there are innumerable sheep to be brought back, and that to us, and to no one else, are our contemporaries confided. It knows the value of time and will not have it wasted. It insists on punctuality, precision and control. This gives it an appearance of haste—isn't love always impatient? The Legion is indeed in a hurry like a business man who goes straight to the point with no digression. But it keeps free from feverish activity. It makes use of all available methods, but it does not make idols of them: it trusts in God alone through these methods and means.

Just a few more steps . . . and we reach the appointed end. 'Yet a little while,' said Jesus, 'and you shall see Me.' Then and not before shall we be entitled to rest. Till then we make our own the fighting prayer of St. Ignatius:

'Grant me, O Lord, to serve Thee as Thou desirest,
To give and not to count the cost,
To fight and not to heed the wounds,

> To labour and not to ask for rest
> To spend myself and not to seek reward
> Save that of knowing I do Thy Will.'

Till then we pray to our Queen that she may uphold us with her beauty and her glory. With our Eastern brethren, we shall salute her with the hymn of our trust and admiration:

> Hail to thee wonder of angel song;
> Hail to thee acceptable incense of prayer;
> Hail to thee purification of the universe;
> Hail to thee living image of the sacred fonts;
> Hail to thee scent of the perfumes of Christ;
> Hail to thee holy one, holier than the holy;
> Hail to thee monstrance of Christ;
> Hail to thee ruin of devils.
>
> <div align="right">(From the <i>Acathist hymn</i>).</div>

Just a few more steps ... and we can say to God: *Ostende faciem tua et salvi erimus.* 'Shew us Thy face and we shall be saved' (*Ps.* 89, 4). For it is to this vision face to face that we are called, and only the glory of God as He is in Himself can fully satisfy our souls. *Satiabor cum apparuerit gloria tua.* There in the Holy Trinity will be fulfilled our destiny, that is, God's plan for our lives. Christ came to us that we might have 'access both in one Spirit to the Father.' (*Eph.* 2, 18). There exist no other lasting riches, no other fullness of life. There is no greater desire that we can make our own, according to St. Paul: 'The grace of Our Lord Jesus Christ and the charity of God and the communication of the Holy Ghost be with you all.' (2 *Cor.* 13, 13).

Imagine how close was the communion with the Holy Trinity, even here on earth, experienced by Mary.

How her union with the Holy Spirit and with Jesus was to lead to the final stage, union with the Father.

For did she not bear in time Him whom the Father begets from all eternity?

In common with Him had she not that only Son of whom she could say: *Ego hodie genui te*, 'Today have I begotten Thee'?

No one shared as she did in the fruitfulness of God, and in His desire to deliver up the Son of God for the salvation of the world.

The life of Christ is but an enduring act of oblation to His Father. How could Mary's life not be caught up in this same current? St. Ignatius of Antioch in the depths of his heart heard a voice, like the murmur of running water, repeating 'Come to the Father.' Mary's life is but a continuing fidelity to this behest as it became increasingly pressing, harder to resist till it reached its final completion in the ecstasy of the Assumption.

This Trinitarian life we can live even here below: for Heaven lies beyond baptism, not death. In the waters of baptism we passed from death to life, from the death of sin to eternal life. We now share in this life of the Trinity and with the familiarity of children can truly associate ourselves with the mutual delight of the divine Persons in their living union. But as yet we hold these joys, these treasures, in fragile vessels, on earth we experience only the first glimmers of that eternal dawn. That is why we must lift our heads to Heaven and be on watch for the dawn. This will help us to walk in darkness, to hasten on and overcome our lassitude. *In domo Domini ibimus*. We are on our way to our Father's house, we are only camping for the night in this earthly country, as we cross it. Our Father is waiting to overwhelm us with His joy and love. When, at the final halting place, we fall into His arms —*in sinu Patris*—we shall realize that no sacrifice could be too great a price to pay for such an encounter, ending in an eternal Magnificat.

CHAPTER VIII.

PRAYER AND ACTION

CONFIDENT, THAT THOU WILT SO RECEIVE ME—AND USE ME—AND TURN MY WEAKNESS INTO STRENGTH THIS DAY, I TAKE MY PLACE IN THE RANKS OF THE LEGION, AND I VENTURE TO PROMISE A FAITHFUL SERVICE. I WILL SUBMIT FULLY TO ITS DISCIPLINE, WHICH BINDS ME TO MY COMRADES, AND SHAPES US TO AN ARMY, AND KEEPS OUR LINE AS ON WE MARCH WITH MARY.

'*I venture to promise a faithful service.*'
What exactly does the Legion ask of those who join it?
'The object of the Legion of Mary,' answers the Manual, right at the beginning, 'is the sanctification of its members *by prayer and active co-operation*, under ecclesiastical guidance, in Mary's and the Church's work of crushing the head of the serpent and advancing the reign of Christ.'

Its rule can thus be expressed in two words, prayer and work: *Ora et labora*, the monastic motto. Those are its orders, summing up its requirements. It is with them that the promise of fidelity should comply.

1. *Prayer.*

Ora. Pray. A primordial duty which admits no argument: a Christian should pray as he breathes.

Because God is God, and at every instant we must recognize the fact.

Because Jesus told us to pray without ceasing.

Because without prayer we are doomed to helplessness.

There is no need to insist on this duty, common to all. But

what, it will be asked, does the Legion lay down as its programme of prayer?

Here a distinction must be made between the various grades. To those who come with a novice's goodwill it prescribes no rigid formula, for it wishes to open its ranks to the ordinary Catholic who is willing to offer loyal service. It welcomes him and makes allowances for the particular circumstances of his life, whether he be tramp or Member of Parliament, street-cleaner or University professor. As a pledge of his goodwill it demands his regular attendance at the weekly meeting where he will find himself in an atmosphere of closely mingled prayer and action. Gradually the practice of apostolic union with Mary will open his soul imperceptibly to breathing in union with her which will become one and the same as breathing in the Holy Spirit. He will experience a hunger and thirst gnawing at him. Without wise words or exposition of the mechanism of prayer he will find that, in practice, union with Mary will progressively lead him into a state of union with God, the very end and object of prayer. This growth will vary according to the grace granted to each individual, *secundum mensuram donationis Christi*. Experience shows that Mary's service is a safe school of authentic prayer.

But if, at the beginning, the Legion imposes no formula of prayer upon its members—save the catena, the short prayer obligatory upon all—it has constantly before its eyes the ideal to which it hopes to lead all its members, no matter what stage they start from. Its ambition is to get them to accept as a rule of life, daily Mass and Communion, daily recitation of some Office, or part of the Breviary, and the Rosary.

Mass, Communion, Office, Rosary: such is the programme proposed for laymen of the Legion, such the portion of prayer that the Legion desires for all.

The Holy Eucharist, the Food of Personal Life.

We need not repeat here all that daily Mass and Communion mean in Christian life. *Si scires donum Dei*! If the faithful knew what a great gift God has put within our reach, and what the Holy Eucharist is, what life-giving strength they would draw from it. Mass, with Communion, which completes it, is the sacrifice of perfect adoration, *Adoramus Te*, we adore Thee; of thanksgiving, *gratias agimus Tibi propter magnam gloriam Tuam*. We give Thee thanks for Thy great glory; of pardon, *qui tollis peccata mundi miserere nobis*, Thou that takest away the sins of the world, have mercy upon us; of intercession *qui tollis peccata mundi, suscipe deprecationem nostram*, Thou that takest away the sins of the world, receive our prayer.

By uniting ourselves to it each morning, we give to God the best we can offer Him: the Body and Blood of the perfect Victim. No earthly act is higher; it is a matchless gift, a thanksgiving rising from earth to Heaven worthy of God.

There is no more universal nor more fruitful gift, for at all times and to all peoples it distributes the infinite merits of our Redeemer's death. The sacrifice of the Mass is the sacrifice of the Cross multiplying its effects of grace: 'The Eucharist is the perfect sacrament of the Passion of the Lord inasmuch as it contains the self-same Christ who suffered.'([35]) And at the same time we are associated with the compassion of Mary, *consors Passionis*, said the Fathers of the Church. Since, through the sacrifice of the altar we climb to Calvary, we find there Our Lady and the mystery of her effective participation in the suffering of her Son.

Indeed, what deeply marks the Legionary at the beginning of his day is his union with Mary in the sublime meeting-place that is the Mass.([36]) Who better than she can initiate her children into the Eucharistic mystery? It is for Our Lady of the Precious Blood to teach us to understand the value of that Blood which was shed and which sprang from her heart. Hers to make us share the sentiments of her Son when He made the supreme sacrifice.

No one is associated as she is with the sacrifice. She stood on Calvary to ratify in our name the redeeming death of her Son. She brought Him her 'compassion,' that is to say the highest union of soul that earth can offer to God, an unbounded adherence to the will of God and the work of salvation. Forgetful of self, Mary entered into this mystery of death and life with peerless faith. Through the wounds and the agony of His death, she perceived and adored the mystery of salvation taking place before her eyes. Even in her tears, the evidence of her incomparable love of God and men, she united herself unreservedly to the Redemption of the world, and as never before, abandoned herself to the love of God.

No one better than she could immerse us in that adoration, expiation and ransom.

The Legionary will unite himself with her sacrifice just as he unites himself with her Communion. What security is his to be able to offer to Jesus the heart and welcome of His Mother, to leave her to receive her Son in our place.

'After Holy Communion,' wrote St. Louis-Marie de Montfort, 'You should introduce Jesus into the heart of Mary. You should present Him to His Mother, who will receive Him lovingly, place Him honourably, adore Him profoundly, love Him perfectly, embrace Him closely, and offer Him in spirit and in truth many tokens of homage that are unknown to us in our impenetrable darkness.' (*True Devotion*, 270).

How blessed is this substitution of her for us; how it puts us at our ease! It is enough for me to know that they are together under my roof, that Mary will speak for me, and will teach me the silence of God. How far this takes us from our wretched thanksgivings, so full of deficiencies, so paltry and self-centred. I have something far better to give to the Lord than my own poor, cold, changeable feelings. No need now to be afraid of coming to Him empty-handed, offering less even than the stable at Bethlehem. To anyone who complains of his neediness Jesus might answer: I ask nothing but the heart of My Mother.

Offering to Him Mary's heart all burning for His glory, our souls will become increasingly consumed with missionary zeal and our personal Communion will be so broadened as to include the whole world. It will be continued by means of courageous, faithful, apostolic action, which is the only trustworthy thanksgiving.

What strength, also, for the Legionary nourished on this food. No need to fear for him the fatigues of the journey. He will undertake all his duties as a Christian, like the prophet *in fortitudine cibi illius*, with the strength of this food and drink. Mary will see him go without anxiety, like a mother who knows her children to be robust and will not fall by the way. May no Legionary ever voluntarily omit, even on one day, this life-giving Communion.

The Holy Eucharist the End and Means of the Apostolate.

Mary not only wishes us to be nourished on the Body and Blood of her Son; furthermore, she desires us to go out into the highways and bye-ways and invite many to this feast of the Lamb. In one sense the whole Catholic apostolate converges on the altar and the communion rail. This ceaseless pursuit of the lost sheep has no other aim than to bring men to the Sacraments of regeneration and life. 'Except you eat the flesh of the Son of man and drink His blood you shall not have life in you.' (*John* 6, 54). The Legionary longs to see all his fellows live henceforward by this eternal life. Could there be a finer or more maternal mission? And what a reward will the faithful servant receive when the Master says to him, 'I was hungry and you gave me to eat: I was thirsty and you gave me to drink.' Happy those who held out to their unknown brother this Bread and this Chalice.

Think on Mary's gratitude to one who has fed her starving children with this Bread of life.

The Manual adds a valuable reflection. It invites the Legionary to make of the Holy Eucharist an instrument of conversion, a lure to draw men, in search of God. Show then, it says, this God so close, within reach of their lips and hands, and perhaps they will then understand how far the love of God surpasses their boldest dreams. May the Eucharist cease to be for them the stumbling-block it was for the disciples, but a call to faith. Is that a paradox? Only seemingly so; for if God is love, the religion revealed by Him is bound to lead us ever deeper into His heart. Could any invention of love and friendship be more wonderful than the Eucharist?

In his life of Mgr. Dupanloup, E. Faguet tells us how a young convert was brought to give up Protestantism and adopt the Catholic faith on account of the Eucharist. What, together with celibacy, had seemed to her to provide the greatest obstacle to joining the Church, all at once became the very clearest motive for believing. She ends the account of her conversion thus: 'The Catholic Church possesses the Eucharist, the total gift of God to man; the Church engenders virginity, the total gift of man to God. I believe there is the greatest truth where is the greatest love.'

These words are far-reaching in consequence. This example should help us to understand why the Manual can dare to say 'By holding this culminating glory of the Church constantly before the eyes of our separated brethren, we shall force them to recognize the real Presence, at least as possible, and then the best of them will say to themselves: "If this be true what a fearful privation I have so far endured." This agonizing thought will provoke the first serious move towards their true home.'

So the Legionary will make himself the willing herald of the supreme love shown by God who loved us 'to the end.' His apostolate would not be truly Marian if it were not Eucharistic.

The Divine Office.

The Legion believes in the transcendent value of the Church's prayer. Consequently it invites its members to adopt as a daily practice, either a considerable part of the breviary (Matins and Lauds, for instance, or the Day Hours) or some office approved by the Church.

It does not lay down any precise programme of mental prayer

because here lies open the whole field of individuality, and this differs from soul to soul. It conforms to the traditional practice of the Church. It deems it sufficient to invite the Legionary to draw fully from this Divine Office, at one time the common possession of monks and layfolk, for the Legion is wholly convinced that nothing equals the Church's own prayer as a means of endowing her children with the true mentality of their mother. That they may think with the Church—*sentire cum Ecclesia*—it urges them to pray with the Church, with her lips and in her words. It knows that the voice of the Bride has a special effect upon the heart of the Bridegroom and that she alone knows the best words to use and the tone of voice that is fitting. For the Holy Ghost Himself inspired the Psalms which form basis of the office, so that on a final analysis, it is He who animates this prayer.

The Legionary should recite them in union with the Church or with Mary: it is the same thing. Moreover, Mary knows the psalms. When on earth she made them the food of her soul. Let us join our prayer with that of our mother. She bends to hear our faltering words. She takes our petitions and makes their very terms holy. She raises them up as a sacrifice of praise which God cannot resist.

For through the voice of Mary, Christ speaks, pleads, sings. The union between Mother and Son is such that to pray in Mary is the surest way of praying in Jesus Christ. To unite ourselves with her heart, to rely on her is to enter ever more deeply into the heart of her Son, and draw down upon ourselves the blessing uttered by God the Father over Jesus: 'This is my beloved Son in whom I am well pleased.'

The Rosary.

To this solemn liturgical prayer, the Legion adds a humbler, more popular form, namely the five, or even fifteen, decades of the rosary. We speak here of both without distinction. It goes without saying that there is no question here of a purely vocal prayer, but of one filled and endowed with life by meditation on the mysteries.

We may pause a moment to discover the hidden soul and portray the spiritual treasures contained in the Rosary, considered in this way, 'Our Lady's Psalter,' as several Popes have described it.

In the first place it should be realized that we are not asked to love the Rosary for its own sake, because we like it, or because we find it pleasant to tell off a string of 'Aves.' Everyone is free to consider this repetition—at first sight—tediously monotonous, or to complain of the inevitable distractions that accompany it.

If the Church asks her children to persevere in it, then it is obviously because this prayer pleases the Queen of Heaven. It is enough for us to know she likes to hear it; everything is contained in that.

Leo XIII published fifteen encyclicals about the Rosary so that none could doubt the lofty position accorded to it by the Church in her prayer.

Pius IX said: 'Give me an army saying the Rosary and I will conquer the world.'

The Legion offers itself to be that army; this weapon is its battle-sword.

The same Pope one day wrote the following lines, a revelation of his own holy soul: 'Of all prayers the Rosary is the loveliest and the richest in grace, the prayer that is most pleasing to the most holy Virgin Mary. Love the Rosary, then, and recite it devoutly every day: this is my last will, which I leave to you that you may remember me.'

These are weighty words, the result of practical experience.

The testimony of the Church and her saints could be multiplied indefinitely. In this commentary on the Promise we prefer to restrict ourselves to showing a particular aspect of the Rosary, namely, as a means of devotion to the Holy Ghost, to whom the Promise is made.

The Rosary is a mystery of communion with the Holy Ghost

Such indeed it appears to those who penetrate its final reality, to those who discover the unity beneath this torrent of praise, to those who grasp the thread which links all the beads.

For that it is sufficient to realize that this prayer is more Mary's prayer than ours; therein lies the key to its power and the charm it exerts on the heart of God. While our fingers tell the beads Our Lady changes the Aves into an ineffable song which Heaven alone can intercept. A change occurs analogous to that effected by our musical instruments. Suppose there is here a gramophone record. I connect it with a small steel needle which at once begins its monotonous round in the grooves of the record. A deaf spectator would make nothing of it, thinking it fruitless and boring. But to those who can hear comes a magnificent voice, they know not how, from this metal needle and ceaselessly turning disc. Soon music swells, filling the room.

That is a remote enough analogy of the substitution which takes place, if in union with Mary I say my beads. As soon as by an act of spiritual union I am united to her, like the needle with the record, and start repeating my *Aves*, Mary takes possession of this movement of prayer and it is she who sings before God in my place and for me, the *Alleluia* of her joy, the *Fiat* of her grief, and the *Amen* of her glory. And all Heaven listens, for Mary repeats to God all the feelings of her heart. This song is a ceaseless communion with the Holy Ghost, effecting in Jesus and in her, all the wonders commemorated by the Rosary. For from the joyful mystery of the Annunciation to the glorious mystery of the Coronation of Our Lady, we witness her remembrance of the culminating moments of her submission to the action of the Holy Ghost.

The Rosary begins with the message of the angel calling on Mary to abandon herself to this action.

It is the start of a wonderful story. At every stage of the existence of the most blessed Virgin we can admire the impulse which bears her towards every manifestation of the Divine will, which in joy, in sorrow, or in glory are shown to her by the Holy Spirit. We are united with that impulse. We witness the growing activity of her soul. She unites herself ever more closely with the mystery of love that the workings of God make manifest in her, in darkness as in light, in death and in resurrection. She knows that God is love; that is certainty enough. Never was there more perfect abandonment. The nails and the blood, the crown of thorns, the cross, Calvary itself, are all of them to her means of communion with the Holy Spirit. She co-operates with the Divine Spirit in the sacrifice of her own Son. She remains faithful to Him right beyond the tomb. And it is this faithfulness which, at last, on the threshold to eternity, is crowned by the glorious Assumption.

While we tell our beads and watch each of the mysteries unfolding before us, Mary, hearing us, obtains for us the grace to enter into this communion with the Holy Ghost. Taking us by the hand she leads us to Him.

Because the Rosary thus becomes the Canticle of Canticles of the Holy Ghost and Mary, we have perhaps no better method of continually reawakening and deepening our devotion to the Holy Spirit. Its hidden riches inspired Georges Goyau to write, in its praise, words which seem strange only to those whose superficiality prevents their penetrating to the heart of a humble recitation of the Rosary:—

> 'This prayer which seems merely verbal is the most spiritual of all;
> This prayer which seems slavish repetition is the freest of all;
> This prayer which seems elementary is the most contemplative of all.'[37]

The paradox is resolved for those who understand how this prayer charms the heart of Mary. Is not every 'Hail Mary' 'A chaste loving kiss given to Mary, a crimson rose presented to her, ambrosia and a cup of nectar prepared for her?' (St. Louis-Marie de Montfort).

In the light of all this, it is easy enough to understand why the Manual says of the Rosary that 'it is to the Legionary meeting as breath is to the body.' (38)

2. *Action.*

'*I venture to promise a faithful service.*'

Faithful to prayer. Faithful also to the accepted task. *Ora et labora.* The Legionary knows that God is counting on his help to complete the Redemption of mankind.

Apostolic action—necessary to the work of God.

This apostolic service is just as indispensable to God as the matter of the Sacraments. Without water there can be no baptism. Without bread and wine there is no Body and Blood of Jesus. God, of His positive will, has linked the grace He gives in baptism, as also the wonder of consecration, with dependence on the presence of these indispensable elements. It is the same with the salvation of the world. God has entrusted men with this task. Normally without their visible and tangible co-operation, salvation will not be passed on. It needs a gesture on our part. Such is the scope and need of the legionary apostolate. For the Legionary, faithful service means going out at night when he would rather be resting peacefully at home; it means knocking at this or that door not knowing what kind of a reception he will get; it means braving bad weather and the irony or coldness of people who have something else to do than to bother with their eternal salvation; it means accepting snubs with a smile, winning entry to homes by force of kind and humble patience; it means sharing the burdens of his brothers and becoming their friends. . . .

Faithful service means offering oneself to a many-sided apostolate, in all forms, foreseen or unforeseen, with the sole desire, to open up the way for God. It means following the example of those servants at the marriage at Cana who received from Jesus the strange order to fill up the empty jars with water when they needed wine. But it was enough that the order was given to pour water into each jar *usque ad summum*, up to the brim; without understanding the servants obeyed. Just so the Legionary in the course of the work undertaken, offers to the Master the water of his good will, that He may pour over mankind the wine of His redeeming grace. That there is no proportion between His gesture and ours is immaterial. What matters is that we should make the gesture. For God has linked the destiny of one man with another, as a mountain guide coils the rope round each climber, so that the whole group may ascend.

We must not fail God either on the pretence that He can do all, or that silent example is enough. Sometimes the hidden life of the Holy Family at Nazareth is taken as authority for refraining from speech and action. To do so is to overlook much; that effacement was a direct response to God's particular desire. Moreover the lives of Jesus, Mary and Joseph, should not be considered as the lives of hermits, given over to pure contemplation. They led the ordinary life of the inhabitants of Nazareth. The custom in the East of good neighbourliness and hospitality is well known. Neighbour chats with neighbour in leisurely fashion. Jesus lived as did the devout Jews, the Anawins, described by the Psalms and Book of Wisdom. This life, however modest, comprised all those works of mercy enumerated in Deuteronomy. It included also prayer, fasts, public acts and pilgrimages. All of which, naturally, led the Holy Family into close contact with others. And are we to think that the first 'Christian' family, living model of all the virtues, practised no zeal for souls or spiritual charity? Admittedly the hour of the Messianic apostolate had not yet struck, but—as the finding of Jesus in the Temple shows—His soul was consumed with zeal and how can the tongue not speak of what fills the heart?

If at all costs the ideal of a purely contemplative life must be sought in the life of Our Lord, we should suggest, at the risk of over-simplification, that the thirty years of the hidden life are the model of ordinary life, the three years of public life, the pattern *par excellence* of Apostolic life when the 'Messianic Kingdom' was established, and the forty days in the desert—the transition from one to the other—the effective image of a life withdrawn and wholly devoted to contemplation.

Fearlessly, then, we repeat: the Christian in the world has no right to take refuge in silence. Speech follows on faith as its direct result. *Repleti sunt omnes Spiritu Sancto et coeperunt loqui*, sings the Church in an antiphon at Pentecost. The apostles were filled with the Holy Ghost and began preaching. A logical sequence. 'I believed for which cause I have spoken,' said St. Paul to the Corinthians as though one was a natural consequence of the other. (2 *Cor.* 4, 13).

How do you expect faith to be born, he asked again, unless it be engendered by words: *fides ex auditu*. And how else has the Church spread? 'But the word of the Lord increased and multiplied,' says the Acts speaking of the growing number of new disciples. (*Acts* 12, 24). Shall we deny our origins?

The Gospels tell of crying the truth from the housetops, and of seeing that the light is not hidden under a bushel. An order is heard here which cannot be defied. *Ite, docete omnes gentes.* 'Teach ye all nations.' Such was the positive order given by Jesus to the apostles, the disciples and to all who call themselves His. And to prevent any possible doubt at Pentecost, the Holy Ghost came down in the form of tongues of flame upon those men gathered in the Cenacle.

The silent tongues and closed mouths of modern Catholics are symbolic not of true Catholicism, but of an undervalued religion. The policy of non-intervention can claim no authority from the Master. Rather can those who proclaim the Gospel message too loudly excuse an excess of zeal by the words: *vae mihi si non evangelizavero.* 'Woe unto me if I proclaim not the message.' Or again, *insta opportune, importune, argue, obsecra*: In season and out of season strive to turn men away from fables and make them ready for the saving truth.

Needless to say, not for a moment do we under-estimate the contemplative life to which God calls the choicest souls. Their silence is not emptiness but a fullness, not desertion but action of a different kind, beyond the realm of speech. The centres of prayer to which they withdraw are like great electric transformer stations, receiving high tension current and supplying whole districts. Their Thebaids are indeed arsenals of grace; but soldiers are still necessary who will be willing to use these weapons and stand up in battle agains the enemy. It is to these soldiers that we are speaking, to all Christians living in the world whose duty it is to wield the sword of the Word of God, and visibly to extend His kingdom. To the Christians of his time who were afraid to answer the summons, St. John Chrysostom addressed these ever-relevant words: 'Among other duties you have that of devoting yourselves to the salvation of your brethren, of leading them to us despite their resistance, cries and complaints. Their opposition and indifference are proof that you are dealing with children. It is for you to change the imperfect and sorry disposition of their souls. It is your duty to coax them to become, in effect, men.'

In spite of these pressing reproaches which are meant to break down our reluctance, we still do not confess ourselves beaten: with all our ingenuity we seek to evade the peremptory commands which cut to the quick.

Apostolic Action, a Universal Duty.

Be an apostle. But that is too great a task for us! we exclaim. 'It is only saints who save the world . . . and we aren't saints. . . . Don't push us into impossible undertakings.' What a strange evasion, and how it conceals fear and cowardice under the convenient veil of a false modesty. Certainly, saints are required to convert the world. May Heaven provide them in abundance for our world in distress. Giants are needed to face the unleashed powers of Hell. We need an Augustine, a Boniface, a Francis, a Dominic, a Vincent Ferrier, an Xavier, miracle workers and prophets. And we need the saints who hid themselves in desert places, far from the world, to belong only to God, in order to belong the more to us. But, it must not be inferred from this, we repeat, that only saints have the care of souls or are responsible for the salvation of their brethren. Moreover, there must be no mistake: sanctity is no far-off inaccessible height, like some inviolable Alpine peak which it is hopeless to think of climbing. In fact, every baptized Christian came forth sanctified from the baptismal waters. In a very real sense—which was usual with St. Paul and the early Church—we have not to become but to remain saints. We have to make wide use of the grace and sanctity received at the beginning. Strictly speaking, it is not because we imitate Our Lord that we become holy, but because we are holy—through our baptism—that we have to imitate Him. And our very imitation of Christ is not a copy produced exteriorly, it is Christ Himself working within us—so greatly does His holiness penetrate us—when with all our strength we reach towards Him. We have no right to disregard our origin: *agnosce, christiane, dignitatem tuam*. So we can conclude that 'noblesse oblige' and that the race of saints is no stranger to us. This will help us to understand that the duty of the apostolate is inherent in our souls, as is the seal of the sacrament by which we were born into life.

If it were only the saints who had this duty to fulfil, the Popes, who so insistently call the laity to the apostolate, would be asking the impossible. Now, God claims for His service every bit of goodwill. Each one of us, whatever his degree of personal virtue, can and ought to be a tool in His hands. God makes use of us all and His grace will uplift us. With and in Him we far exceed our own capacity. There are some graces which God gives to this or that man, however ignorant or unworthy. All theologians speak of graces 'entirely gratuitous' *gratis datae*, to describe those graces which do not necessarily make the recipient holy, but are destined by God for the community, through the medium of a particular individual. The *charismata* of the early Church are a striking example of this; one received the gift of speaking in tongues unknown even to himself, and another the power to interpret them for the good of all. God does not limit His generosity to our receptivity, any more than a fountain limits its flow to the size of our vessels or our thirst. But He desires that every man should allow himself to be filled with Him and overflow. Moreover, all sacramental theology implies this sovereign independence of the grace of God, which carries on its work, even if the priest who administers is in a state of grievous sin. We should thank God who does not allow Himself to be limited by our weakness, and triumphs despite our crimes.

In union with Mary, the Legionary, in spite of his own unworthiness, will find the means to be constantly overflowing with grace. It is enough for him to be united with her, that he, too, may be at every moment, 'full of grace.' . . . From this inexhaustible wealth, he may give and give again without ever impoverishing himself. In spite of his own poverty he possesses from that moment wealth enough to enrich all whom God has put in his path.

The apostolate, then, is not the monopoly of the most virtuous. It is an obligation on us all, a blessed obligation that God has made imperative yet possible, sublime, but within our reach. The devil, forced out of this position, is still by no means short of crippling arguments. For the benefit of our contemporaries, fonder of freedom than truth, he continually spreads about an insidious slogan. The apostolate, he whispers, is an attempt upon the independence of our neighbour, a violation of his conscience. So it happens that Catholics admire the missionary who goes off to convert the Eskimo, yet blames one who at home desires to save his neighbour's soul. To urge that the apostolate is an intrusion, makes nonsense of the words of the Master, 'going, therefore, teach ye all nations.' Grant that ignorant good faith is the equivalent of theological faith and the very foundation of all missions crumbles. Doubtless God possesses treasures of mercy for those who know no better than to worship fetishes. But for them also He holds in reserve treasures of superabundant divine life of incomparable richness, and He desires that all men should live by it and that we should take this divine life to them. Certainly we must not constrain the conscience of others, nor seize them by main force. But there are 'words of life' which we have no right to keep to ourselves, even though our neighbour does not in the least suspect their blessedness. In the category of spiritual charity there are sins of omission graver than all others, on which God will judge us. And above all, dominating every other duty, the glory of God must be accomplished through us so that the petitions of the Lord's Prayer may be heard and find expression in action: 'Thy kingdom come, Thy will be done on earth, as it is in Heaven.' In speaking of the missionary obligation, the Church does not think primarily of men, but of God. St. Ignatius, to stir up his young religious for the struggle, wrote these burning words, dominated by the thought of God: 'Where today is the majesty of our God adored? Where is His power respected? Where are His infinite goodness and patience known?' However, much out of tune with the times, this is the only kind of language compatible with that of the Gospels. It teaches us that not only must God be given to men, but men must be given to God, and open their hearts to His mystery.

But still people do not confess themselves beaten. The objection is repeated in new terms: to be an apostle is the task of the cultivated, the well-educated. 'I have not the requisite knowledge to undertake such a role.' That is but another evasion, just as specious and worthless as the last. God has not confined the apostolic duty to a few learned professors. His choice of twelve fishermen of Galilee, certainly does not suggest that high intellectual standing is an indispensable requirement to found the Kingdom of God. There is even a passage in the Gospel where Jesus cried out with joy because it had pleased the Father to reserve to children and the humble the secret hidden from the wise and prudent. Besides, the history of the Church shows us that the greatest number of conversions have been effected by simple men: slaves, artisans, soldiers, travellers. The learned have come in their turn, but they were not the first, any more than the Magi were first at the Crib. All that is needed to convince one's neighbour is a real and sincere faith; and to talk to him on equal terms will ever be the normal way to touch his heart. Of course at a later stage, when advanced religious instruction is needed, or difficult objections have to be met, recourse to the specialist will be necessary. But as a rule that is not the first step. The faith is not disclosed by a volley of syllogisms. Must the words of St. Paul to the Corinthians be repeated? 'There are not many wise according to the flesh, not many mighty, nor many noble. But the foolish things of the world hath God chosen, that He may confound the wise; and the weak things of the world hath God chosen that He may confound the strong. And the base things of the world and the things that are contemptible, hath God chosen; and things that are not that He might bring to naught things that are: that no flesh should glory in His sight.' (1 *Cor*. 1, 26-29).

The idea of seeking to recruit Legionaries from the lower classes and the simple folk, at least as much as from other classes is very dear to the Legion, for it asserts a vital principle of Catholicism, namely that all members of the Church, even the most ordinary, are called to the apostolate. This truth has been obscured and generally there is a temptation to seek recruits among the spiritually advanced or the intellectually cultured. This is to forget that God makes an exception of nobody, and that He calls all the world to indispensable action.

More than ever is this true nowadays. Who is not familiar with the appeal of H.H. Pope Pius XII to the men of Italian Catholic Action (Sept. 7, 1947)? 'The time for thinking and planning has passed: the hour for action has come. Are you ready? The forces opposing each other in the religious and moral sphere become daily more sharply defined: the time of testing is here. The swift race of which St. Paul spoke has begun: now is the time for intense effort. Merely a few moments may determine the victory.'

Strenuous Apostolic Action.

Now is the time for intense action.

The Legion attaches special importance to intense loyal service. A whole chapter of the Manual is devoted to 'Intensity of effort in Mary's service.' Without in any way minimizing the function of grace, it is important to be keenly aware of the need for effort of this kind. That we are useless servants, and fellow-workers with God is the complete truth, every aspect of which must be continually maintained. Union with Mary, which is a lasting dependence experienced to the full and a constant breathing in by the soul of the Holy Ghost, will preserve the Legionary from the snares of quietism, or of a naturalist activity. But it will teach him, too, the value of effort.

In his Encyclical on the Mystical Body—as in that on the Liturgy—H.H. Pius XII insists on the danger of the Quietist temptation, reminding us that St. Ambrose said, 'The blessings of God are for those who bestir themselves, not for those who slumber.' And he asks us to meditate on the teaching of St. Paul who lays down on the one hand: 'If I live it is not I who live, but Christ who lives in me,' but who is not afraid to say at the same time, 'God's grace has not been idle in me. I have worked more than all they: but it is not I but the grace of God with me.'

It is not uncommon to meet Christians who seem too sparing of effort in carrying out their apostolic duties and who excuse themselves by saying 'Personally I can do nothing: I rely entirely on God.' As though this lack of vision, work and method, were the expression of the highest virtue of abandonment. It must be stated without equivocation: indolence is no homage to God, inaction is no way to draw down graces. To prove this we have only to read the parable of the buried talents in the Gospel. It is a cunning temptation to reason from the premise 'without me thou canst do nothing,' and so arrive at the false conclusion that one must remain with folded arms. This is to forget that God must be loved and served with all one's heart, with all one's soul, and with all one's strength, not merely with lip service. It is a misunderstanding of the value that God Himself has set upon our efforts and of the law established by His Providence, which makes our efforts normally indispensable. Jesus, with His all-powerful love, is there in the tabernacle. Nonetheless, if no priest comes that way to open the tabernacle door and give the Host to those who wish to communicate, the sacramental grace will not be theirs. God has willed to have need of men. And since this is His plan, and we are His tools, we must needs work to the limit of our powers. Devotion to Mary in apostolic action is synonymous with work well and truly done with energy, skill and quality. It is unseemly that we should wait for the Queen of Heaven to make up for deficiencies due to our own lack of effort. Our generosity should always equal our confidence, and the latter never dispenses from the former.

Above all, we must never be afraid of doing too much. Were we, in a given case, to do ten times more than was necessary, Mary would gather up the surplus and use it in her own good time for some other souls in distress. As the Manual rightly says, 'There is nothing lost of anything which is committed to the hands of the careful housewife of Nazareth.'

We should have, then, no misgivings about the intensity of apostolic action but decidedly we should fear indolence, what is slipshod or left unfinished; God is worthy of better than that. As none other, Mary has a concern for work well done, and it cannot be imagined that in her life on earth, she was satisfied to offer God half-measures.... From us she expects active, imaginative, collaboration, the kind that takes things to heart. We owe her our greatest efforts: he who has given less than everything has so far given nothing, and when we give we must give always of our best. When she sees that we have done our uttermost, then is the moment to expect everything from her, miracles included if need be. But our courage must be as unlimited as our gift.

Disciplined Apostolic Action.

Faithful service, therefore disciplined service. How many efforts for good have been wasted through lack of cohesion and disordered fighting. The Legion means army, and an army is worth what its discipline is worth. By means of discipline, each individual's effort is incorporated, supported and raised to its highest power. Obedience is the sole condition, and that in clear, precise and controlled fashion. Not seldom people are put off by the earnestness of the Legion which on this point is unyielding. It prefers for God's battery a handful of completely devoted men to a disunited cohort. Rather the three hundred soldiers of Gideon, than an army of mercenaries of doubtful loyalty.

Obedience is strength.

It is also a grace.

For it ensures the freedom of divine intervention. We will explain this. We are by no means obliged to think that our superiors always make the wisest and most considered decision, although there would be some presumption in assuming that they make more mistakes than we do. It is not the object of obedience to enable us to perform the most perfect outward actions, but, as Zundel well says, 'so to keep us in God's hands that He may be able to express Himself in us, in ways beyond anything we are capable of understanding or doing.'[39]

The authority giving orders, then, will appear like the sacrament of our purity of intention, the road open for God's entry in the work in hand. To obey is to surpass oneself, to offer to God a fresh usefulness and a love more chastened and so more complete. Obedience is a guarantee and a safeguard against ourselves.

Against human inconstancy the Legion imposes a weekly meeting.

Against vagueness it imposes the duty of rendering a detailed account of work done.

To a formless desire for the apostolate it gives an element of the substantial and foreseen, while leaving to each the initiative to discover and propose others.

It would seem that there is here a remedy for each of the frailties inherent in poor human nature which, thus supported, obtains unhoped for successes.

Lastly, obedience is a joy, for thus we enter into our Saviour's very mission. By accepting the imposed duty, from day to day, the Legionary lives the command: 'Go, teach ye all nations.' By carrying on, in the position and the manner proper to him, the work of the apostles, he merits that divine presence and aid which Jesus promised: 'Lo, I am with you always.' He does not journey alone, at the mercy of his own caprice and guided by his own lights. He has received clear and precise directions. He goes where God sends him, under Mary's guidance. He is glad to respond as did the servants at Cana, to his mother's order. That is why the Promise requires of him, over and above all else, the abandonment of himself into Mary's hands.

> 'I will submit fully to its discipline,
> Which binds me to my comrades,
> And shapes us into an army,
> And keeps our line as we march on with Mary.'

CHAPTER IX.

MARIAN MEDIATIONS

TO WORK THY WILL. TO OPERATE THE MIRACLES OF THY GRACE.

'*To Operate the Miracles of Thy Grace.*' . . .
ALL THE DARING faith of the Legion is contained in this aspiration. It desires to offer itself to the Holy Ghost that He may be enabled to bring forth, even today, the marvels that He worked in Our Lady.

To understand what this alliance between the Holy Ghost and Mary could be in the future, we may consider a moment those Gospel pages which give the best description of the marvel which occurred in the past.

On one page we read of the visit of Mary to her cousin Elizabeth: the early dawn of Marian mediation.

On another we are shown the scene at Pentecost: the sunrise of Marian mediation.

Both enable us to glimpse the extraordinary fruitfulness of this alliance between the Holy Spirit and Mary, and help us to foresee the immeasurable blessings that subsequent ages record.

1. *The early Dawn of Mediation: the Visitation.*

Firstly, the Visitation.

After the message of the Archangel, see how Mary leaves her home and hastens over the hills to see her cousin. She draws near, and at the first sound of her voice, the Holy Ghost fills Elizabeth with light, causing her child to leap for joy. Consider closely and respectfully for a moment, this first instance of Marian mediation recorded in history, this first gleam in a sky which in subsequent ages will glow with splendour. This is the first miracle of grace to occur visibly at Mary's hands. For there is no possible doubt: it is at Mary's approach that the Holy Ghost works and sanctifies.

And it is because Mary brings to the Precursor, hidden in his mother's womb, the sanctifying presence of Jesus. Through her, John received that purification which invested him even then with his office. Through her, he was consecrated as a witness to Christ before being born.

It is striking to observe how, in this first meeting between Christ and His Precursor, all was accomplished through Mary. Jesus desired to give Himself to John through His mother. At the Visitation, the supernatural motherhood of Mary was suddenly revealed: the head of the accursed serpent felt the first blow from the heel of the woman blessed among all women. John was the first conquest of Our Lady, and the pledge of salvation for us all. At the appearance of Our Lady, Satan suffered his sharpest defeat in John's soul, as it was instantly sanctified. In its turn John's movement of joy caused Elizabeth to exult and drew from her a cry of admiration for the Mother of God. It can be said that through John the Baptist, Mary's glory was for the first time proclaimed. A witness to Christ, John is simultaneously a witness to His mother. One never wearies of contemplating this mystery of the Visitation. The little that the Evangelist tells us, reveals unlimited depths; a union of souls, spiritual interaction, and a marvellous introduction to the great mission that now begins.

If this single contact with Mary, if her very first words produced so much—the regeneration of John the Baptist, and the pouring out of light and grace on Elizabeth—what must we think of the days, months and years which were to follow?

This three-months' stay in the house of Zachary must have had a very deep effect upon John the Baptist. Every day was a mystery of spiritual growth. Already, St. Ambrose tells us, John the Baptist in the womb of his mother had the stature of perfect growth in the fullness of Christ. *Elizabeth Zachariae magnum virum genuit*, sings the Church. It is to enhance this supernatural greatness that Mary remained in 'visitation.' ([40])

It is not for us to delve further: the account of the Visitation is the only one that God has entrusted to the pen of the sacred writer. Her other 'visitations,' we shall hear about in Paradise. Through this episode we can divine what Mary's presence must have been for St. Joseph. The alliance between these two privileged souls entrances the heavenly courts: such purity, such depth of self-giving, and such inviolable fidelity to the love of God and Jesus Christ. It is permissible to believe that though the soul of Joseph was directly united to the Holy Ghost who had made the holy patriarch 'a just man,' the Holy Ghost was pleased to mete out his signal graces to him through Mary. None could know better than Joseph the power and gentleness, the extent and delicacy of Our Lady's influence. ([41])

To return to the Precursor, it is quite natural, after all, for him to be one of the Legion's patrons. For his sanctification touches us more nearly, perhaps, than we think. St. John the Baptist necessarily precedes the coming of Jesus. Such is the arrangement of a wonderful Providence whose 'gifts are without repentance.' That order, like the order of Marian mediation, undergoes no change. Hence, in accordance with it, we are all 'visited' by Our Lady, that Christ may come in us.

Fr. Danielou has accurately described the continuing role of the Forerunner: 'If Jesus,' he says, 'is ever "He who cometh" . . . . John is perpetually he who goes before Him, for the economy of the Incarnation in history is continued in His Mystical Body. Just as all grace comes through Mary because she could not have borne Jesus without being she who bears His Mystical Body, so is every conversion prepared by John the Baptist. Moreover, the Fathers taught this. "I believe," wrote Origen, "that the mystery of John is still accomplished in the world. If anyone is to believe in Christ Jesus, the spirit and strength of John must come into his soul and prepare for the Lord a perfect people, making plain the rough ways of the heart and its paths straight. Even today, the spirit and strength of John precede the coming of the Lord." (*Hom. Luc.*, IV, RAUER, p. 29, 1.20–p. 30, 1.8). Since this coming of Christ is a perpetual coming—He is for ever He who cometh in the world and in the Church—there is a perpetual "Advent" of Christ and this Advent is the mission of John the Baptist. It is the special function of John the Baptist to prepare for what is at hand. His special characteristic is to be there, for that immediate preparation which goes before great spiritual or missionary expansion.'([42])

This view of continuity is traditional in the Church.([43]) Bourdaloue in his sermon for the feast of St. John was not afraid to say: 'Between Jesus and St. John the Baptist there is so close a connection that it is impossible properly to know one without the other; and if eternal life consists in knowing Jesus Christ then a part of our salvation consists in knowing St. John.'

Since he came that all might have faith through him, *ut omnes crederent per illum*, every grace of faith presupposes his definitive action. Another consequence is that the mediation of Our Lady which effected such wonders of grace in him is, for us all, a grace of the highest order. Loving him as she did, Mary began to love us: in him she opened up the first way to salvation and redemption for all her children.

Thus, through Mary, was fulfilled the prophecy made by the angel to Zachary when he announced to him the birth of John: 'And he shall be filled with the Holy Ghost even from his mother's womb.' (*Luke* I, 15).

That is not all. At the sound of Mary's voice, Elizabeth, we said, received illuminating grace. Seeing Mary with new eyes she exclaimed: 'Whence is this to me, that the mother of my Lord should come to me?' adding at the prompting of her heart,

'Blessed art thou that hast believed,' and thus beginning that succession of praise which, down the ages, has fulfilled the prophetic words of the Magnificat, proclaiming Mary blessed.

What an astonishing conversation this is between two women unknown to the world, whose words are to span the centuries. This maiden who has just said that she is but the Lord's servant, suddenly, without transition, gives utterance to this entirely improbable prophecy: 'From henceforth all generations shall call me blessed.' It is disconcerting madness or a divine miracle; no alternative remains. And generations have followed, in impressive and swelling chorus, to make their own the cry of Elizabeth and confirm the prophecy.

'Blessed art thou, Mary, that hast believed,' cried Elizabeth. We in our turn would say to Elizabeth herself: 'Blessed art thou, privileged soul, that hast believed that in Mary the Holy Spirit performed great things. Blessed art thou, for it is neither flesh nor blood, but the Holy Spirit which originated in thee this first impulse of devotion to Our Lady.' It was thus the Holy Ghost Himself who originated veneration of Mary, who initiated the litanies and hymns without number which spring up towards her. He it was, too—let it not be forgotten—who put upon her lips the prophecy of the Magnificat, who made her Queen of prophets. When we say in the Creed, *Credo in Spiritum Sanctum qui locutus est per prophetas*, we recall the prophetic action of the Holy Ghost in Mary, and the new and close relationship which united them.

2. *The Sunrise of Mediation: Pentecost.*

This alliance between the Holy Spirit and Mary, sealed by the Incarnation, already glimpsed as the source of grace in the account of the Visitation, stands out in high relief in the mystery of Pentecost which comes as the conclusion of the Gospel.

Mary is there in the Cenacle, in the midst of the apostles, awaiting the fulfilment of her Son's promise. 'All these were persevering with one mind in prayer with . . . Mary, the mother of Jesus.'

This mention of Our Lady's presence far surpasses the implication of a mere historical detail. It is not without reason that the sacred writer, always so reticent in speaking of Our Lady, emphasizes that she was there. It was necessary for Mary to be at the Cenacle at that important time when the Church was to be born and manifested to the world. She had to be there to receive the expected outpouring of the Holy Ghost upon the apostles.

In one of His Encyclicals, Leo XIII brings out clearly this special and unique place of Our Lady: 'The Blessed Virgin at the Cenacle,' he wrote, 'praying with and for the Apostles with "yearnings unspeakable" prepares and hastens the full and varied gifts to the Church from the Consoling Spirit, which is Christ's supreme gift, never to fail His Church.' (*Jucunda semper*, September 8, 1894).

It was a presence of unique importance not only for the apostles, who were to be transformed, but for the whole world which, thanks to them, receives the first fruits of salvation. Already at Christmas, Mary had given to the world Him who had come to bring fire upon earth and wills that it kindle. Her role would not have been complete without her presence at the Cenacle where the Spirit of her Son was to come to inflame them with that fire which will not be put out until the end of the world.

'Pentecost,' it has been said, 'was the spiritual Bethlehem of Mary, her new Epiphany; as a mother standing by the crib of the Mystical Christ, she made Him known again to other shepherds and other kings.' (Sheen).

Everything in Mary's life is a connected whole; what to us is a succession of apparently isolated episodes fits into God's plan, which is always consistent, and allows just enough to be guessed for us to stand wondering at the unity of His work. For those who can see, the mediation of Pentecost sends down its roots into the very mystery of the Incarnation.

By virtue of this profound unity, Mary has her place at the very heart of the apostolate; she is its queen. If she does not travel the earth to reveal her Son, yet her zeal is as great 'as the sand that is on the sea shore.' (3 *Kings* 4, 29).

She practises the apostolate in an eminent manner. 'Mary,' as M. Olier so accurately said, 'does not perform outwardly the function of an apostle, although she received with the apostles the Spirit of Jesus Christ the universal Apostle, and received it in its fullness. She is not concerned with Jew or Gentile in particular: but having within herself the fullness of her Son's zeal and power over the Church, she possesses also, through her eminent participation in Jesus Christ, both the zeal for God's glory and the power to send secretly, by the channels of the Holy Ghost and divine love, God's servants throughout the world.'

From this angle we can understand better the degree of unity between Mary and apostolic action. Whoever truly unites himself to Mary, emerges from the Cenacle to set out on the conquest of the world. He understands that he has not received the Holy Ghost without also receiving from Him the impulse to the apostolate. *Accipe Spiritum Sanctum*. 'Receive the Holy Spirit,' says the consecrator to the one he consecrates bishop. This formula of consecration constitutes the apostle in the fullest sense of the word. By analogy the same is true of the ordinary Christian: Confirmation—the sacrament which gives him the Holy Ghost, completing the outpouring begun at baptism—consecrates him as an apostle in his place in the world within his own sphere of action.

To refuse to pass on this divine fire is to betray the Holy Ghost and to repudiate Our Lady. Woe betide him who hides his light under a bushel or allows the fire to be covered with ashes. Everyone in his own degree is responsible for the light or darkness pervading the world, for the warmth which kindles it, or the cold which chills it. Though we have not seen tongues of fire descend upon our heads, we know that the Holy Spirit, *sermone ditans guttura*, has given to our voices the power to convince our brothers of the blessings of Redemption. Tongues of flame and a rushing mighty wind are not symbols of inaction, nor of quietude. We honour Mary for her loyalty to the Holy Ghost, when we open our souls to that Divine Spirit in order that we may bear Him to men, our brethren.

3. *The broad Daylight of Mediation at the present Day.*

Here lies the whole ambition of the Legion: to offer generous souls to the action of the Holy Ghost, so that Pentecost may continue in our time: that the Holy Spirit may renew the disfigured face of the earth, and establish His dominion over all things.

Obviously it is an immense ambition, but one founded on faith itself. Jesus Himself said to His disciples: 'And behold, I am with you all days, even unto the consummation of the world . . . you will do greater deeds than I!' These words dominate the whole reality of history. And even now God is ready to operate the miracles of grace and renew the world. This He has told us on the strength of words by which He appears to be bound; He has laid upon us the obligation of hoping for the 'impossible.' But Faith can move mountains. 'With God all things are possible.' What then, are we waiting for?

Some Catholics, nowadays, seem to think that the age of miraculous mass conversions ended with the passing of the primitive Church. Is what was possible then no longer so today? It is a disturbing question, for faith teaches us that Jesus and His Church are one, that the Head and His body live the same life.

Now, the life of Jesus Christ abounded with miracles: it was His own way of forcing His message on the attention of His contemporaries sunk in earthly pre-occupations and limited to a short-sighted Messianism. Miracles were His challenge to unbelief and His introduction to knowledge of the things of God.

Directly He left the earth miracles, we may notice, continued. The shadow of St. Peter cured the lame man at the gate of the Temple and the apostles confirmed their testimony by wonders which roused the Sanhedrin. He was with them as He had promised. His Presence shone forth. The power of God was in the hands of these men who claimed to follow Him and Simon Magus wanted to buy it from them at a high price.

It is, therefore, 'normal' for God to work wonders among

men. It is not He who has arbitrarily decided to make them rare. Yet miracles are rare today. Why?

Is God's arm foreshortened?

Has His love grown weary?

Does our distress no longer move Him?

No, such doubts would be blasphemy. God is God. He is unchanging. His love remains identical with Himself.

Once more then, how can the infrequency of miracles be explained?

Faith: the Source of Grace.

Is it not, perhaps, because God no longer finds among us enough men daring to believe in Him to the length of expecting miracles? Because on our highways He does not meet enough centurions to draw from Him the admiring cry: *Non inveni tantam fidem in Israel*; 'I have not found so great faith in Israel'? Because He finds no Canaanite woman to draw from Him the miracle they implore? Yet the Master is always ready to answer us as He did of old. 'Go, and it shall be done unto thee according to thy Faith.'

Alas! We are bent on seeking the salvation of the world in some limited resource of human wisdom. The prize is his who can draw up original and untried theories of the apostolate. Where are they who take literally St. John's inspired words: *Haec est victoria quae vincit mundum: fides nostra.* (1 John 5, 4)? Ultimately our victory over the world is in proportion to our faith.

We do not in the least deny the usefulness of techniques of approach, indeed faith itself obliges the Christian to use his intelligence, for the Gospels teach us that charity is an ingenious and inventive virtue. But without faith—a faith which adheres to God in total surrender—the power of God will not be obtained, and we shall flounder helplessly in the face of the powers of evil. Not without reason does the Church repeat to her priests every evening at Compline, St. Peter's injunction: Be on your guard, the devil is prowling about; hold your own against him, be strong in your faith: *cui resistite fortes in fide.* . . .

Can we claim that our faith is strong, well-tempered, really seasoned?

Or must we acknowledge that it has lost its vigour, its first freshness? Unfortunately we cannot with impunity breathe in an environment that is vitiated by the foul air of relativism. We cannot live without danger in an atmosphere of materialism and naturalism which, without our knowing it, penetrates into every pore. Love of truth and worship of God have become weak among men. Are vital truths for which we are not prepared to die still truths in our eyes?

Sin belongs to all ages, but our forefathers when they sinned knew themselves blameworthy, and called their sin by its name. To save ourselves discomfort we no longer plead even extenuating circumstances, we endeavour to justify the sin. That perversion the Church fears above all else. She prays God with great solemnity at the consecration of a bishop 'that he may not confuse darkness with light, nor light with darkness; that he shall not confuse good with evil, nor evil with good.' This petition is intensely relevant for our contemporaries who are so tempted to sin against the light. We must learn afresh that truth alone can set us free, and that unacknowledged falsehood disseminates death.

Our faith has grown weak and this weakness upsets the entire framework of Christianity, for faith is its backbone.

The Fullness of Mary's Faith.

If we do not desire to betray our name as Christians, we need a powerful faith. That is why the Legion invites its members to seek in union with Mary an effective share in that fullness of faith which so entranced Elizabeth: *beata quae credidisti.*

Has there ever been faith to compare with Mary's?

Listen to the description of it given by St. Alphonsus:

'Mary's faith surpassed that of all men and all angels.
She saw her Son in the stable at Bethlehem and yet believed that
    He was the Creator of the world.

She saw Him fleeing before Herod, and she never wavered in her faith that He was the King of Kings.

She saw Him being born, and she believed that He was from everlasting.

She saw Him poor, without even elemental necessities, and nevertheless believed Him to be the Master of the universe.

She saw Him lying on straw in the crib and there adored Him as the all-powerful One.

She saw that He spoke not a word, yet she believed that He was the eternal Wisdom itself.

She heard Him cry, and she believed that He was the joy of Paradise.

And in the end she saw Him die, exposed to all manner of insult, affixed to a Cross, and though the faith of all others was shaken,

Yet Mary persevered in her unhesitating belief that He was God.'

(*Quoted in the Manual*).

It has been said with justice that the whole faith of the nascent Church was concentrated in her soul, and that today in the whole Church militant, there is not more faith than there was in Mary's heart.

Jesus did not have faith: the beatific vision that He enjoyed here below, would necessarily preclude Him from it.

Hence Mary stands before us as the most perfect pattern of faith in a human creature—she has merited that all Christian faith should originate in her, at least in the sense that our faith depends on the witness she bore to the mystery of the Incarnation. As Cardinal Wiseman wrote in his study, 'The Action of the New Testament': 'Take away our Blessed Lady's contribution to the Gospel testimony, efface her testimony to Christianity, and you find not simply a link broken, but the very fastening of the whole chain wanting; not merely a gap, or a break, made in the structure, but the foundation gone. The belief in the wonders wrought in the Incarnation, of ages, and of the world, rests upon one point of testimony, a unit, a single voice—that of the Blessed Virgin Mary.'

All faith, to be pleasing to God, must be founded and modelled on hers.

It should not be thought that because on occasion miracles flashed like lightning through the darkness, the faith of the Blessed Virgin was easier or less meritorious than ours. Though, she received the embassy of the Archangel in person and heard the Christmas angels sing; though Elizabeth, Zachary and Simeon revealed to her its greatness in mysterious words, and the star of Bethlehem shone for her as for the Magi, yet Mary's faith never stopped short in face of any of the extraordinary ways of God. Better than anyone she knew that faith possesses God in an infinitely more certain manner. 'Blessed are those who have not seen and have believed,' her divine Son was to say one day. Mary knew the joy of that dark and hidden faith—*et nox illuminatio mea in deliciis meis.* Her faith does not seek to go beyond what lights Providence has seen fit to bestow: and if, sometimes, God increased their number, she was content to thank Him for it, without murmuring when the light was dimmed and, strangely, the star vanished. She knew only this, to cling in every circumstance to the loving will of God. Never did human creature possess a more naked, virginal faith.

One memorable day, she did not understand the words of her Son; she confessed as much to St. Luke: *et non intellexerunt.* For human faith never had greater obstacles to overcome: after the radiant promise of the Archangel and the heavenly song of Christmas night, what contrasts, and how many of them, followed. For Him who was to be called the Son of God, whose reign was to be everlasting, there was only the straw of the stable, the flight into Egypt, the poor obscurity of Nazareth; the Saviour of the world was dogged by misunderstanding, suspicion, and mockery: and all was completed in the most humiliating catastrophe. But Mary believed in the Word of God; she believed in God. Neither the undistinguished nature of His life, nor the hostility and hatred encountered by supreme Love could upset her faith. Mary, who had so humbly agreed to be partner with God in the Incarnation and who had believed that nothing was impossible with the Most High, never ceased to believe that the divine plan would be fulfilled and was never anxious to know how. Everything for her was a sign of God. In the half-light of faith she beheld Him as in darkness we see myriad stars. Her faith did not need the miracle of the Resurrection. No one has entered deeper into the divine mystery: Mary's fidelity triumphantly underwent every trial. Mary believed, as the Mother of God alone could believe who, as no other, knew what God is. We must ever return to those words of Elizabeth: *Beata quae credidisti*.

Union with the Faith of Mary.

It is right, then, for the Legion to set before us the faith of Mary as an outstanding example. Before sending out its members on their apostolic duties, and so that they may have that faith which produces miracles, the Legion asks them to go down on their knees at the feet of the faithful Virgin. It offers them this prayer, this supreme request for a faith which shall be some response to the fidelity of God:

> Confer, O Lord, on us,
> Who serve beneath the standard of Mary,
> That fullness of faith in Thee and trust in her,
> To which it is given to conquer the world.
> Grant us a lively faith, animated by charity,
> Which will enable us to perform all our actions
> From the motive of pure love of Thee,
> And ever to see Thee and serve Thee in our neighbour;
> A faith, firm and immovable as a rock,
> Through which we shall rest tranquil and steadfast
> Amid the crosses, toils and disappointments of life,
> A courageous faith which will inspire us
> To undertake and carry out without hesitation

Great things for God and the salvation of souls;
A faith which will be our Legion's Pillar of Fire
To lead us forth united—
To kindle everywhere the fires of Divine Love—
To enlighten those who are in darkness and in the shadow
   of death. . . .
To inflame those who are lukewarm—
To bring back to life those who are dead in sin;
And which will guide our own feet in the way of peace
So that—the battle of life over—
Our Legion may reassemble,
Without the loss of anyone,
In the Kingdom of Thy Love and Glory.   Amen.

CHAPTER X.

MARY, THE CHURCH, AND THE WORLD

WHICH WILL RENEW THE FACE OF THE EARTH, AND ESTABLISH THY REIGN, MOST HOLY SPIRIT, OVER ALL.

1. *Mary and the Church in General.*

UNDER THE TITLE 'The Spirit of the Legion,' the Manual sums up in these words the spiritual principles by which it is actuated:

'The spirit of the Legion of Mary is that of Mary herself. Especially does the Legion aspire after her profound humility, her perfect obedience, her angelical sweetness, her continual prayer, her universal mortification, her altogether spotless purity, her heroic patience, her heavenly wisdom, her self-sacrificing love of God, and above all, her faith, that virtue which has alone in her been found in its utmost extent and never equalled.'

In bringing out the full sense of the Promise, our commentary, without seeking to do so, has thrown into relief this exact portrait of Our Lady. It is indeed Mary that we see; no one could mistake her for any other; her features and her tone of voice can be recognized. Now, the whole bearing of a true Legionary should recall Mary and exhale the perfume of her presence.

The more faithful the Legionary to his promise, the more will he give a feeling and living likeness of Our Lady.

The more, also, will he be a loyal and faithful son of the Church. It is of capital importance that this consequence should be realized, though it is not necessarily apparent at first glance. Mary and the Church are not, indeed, two unconnected realities, they are, in some sort, the same mystery envisaged from two different points of view. We speak of 'our holy Mother Church,' just as we speak of 'Mary, our Mother.'

There is no discontinuity between these two mysteries. The tradition which tells us that we are born of the Holy Ghost and of Mary asserts likewise that we are born of the Holy Ghost and of the Church.([44]) Thus St. Leo could say, 'The water of baptism is like a virginal womb, and the same Spirit who came down upon Mary, fills the sacred font,' (*Sermon IV, de Nativ.* n. 3). In these conditions devotion to Mary is indeed devotion to the Church.

The bond between Mary and the Church is so real that Protestants quite naturally deny the Catholic teaching about both Mary and the Church. Scheeben tells us that a Protestant asserts that Catholics defend and glorify in Mary their conception of the Church as Mother and Mediatrix of grace.([45])

In the view of this great theologian there is possibly the same fundamental idea underlying the simultaneous rejection by the various Protestant sects of the dogmas of the Immaculate Conception and Papal Infallibility. In any case, Karl Barth emphasized recently the significance of the coincidence.

This is no place to examine these problems; an indication of them is sufficient to show the connection.

It is not mere chance that the Gospel, always so reticent about Mary, mentions her presence at each of the three stages in the founding of the Church: the Incarnation, the Passion and Pentecost. The mystery of the Church is also a mystery of Our Lady.

In his well-known work, Fr. Terrien, S.J., puts it this way:

'Although both conceived by the Holy Ghost and although this spirit of God made both fruitful, Mary to be Mother of Christ and His members, the Church to bring forth children of adoption, for fear of offending either we should not venture to attribute to the Church the inexpressible fullness of the Holy Ghost which we acknowledge in Our Lady: for the Church herself receives from Mary's fullness as Mary shares in Christ's. . . . That is the meaning of the phrase used by the Fathers "The Church imitates the Mother of Christ;" *Ecclesia imitatur Matrem Christi*. . . . Thus the Son of

God created the Church in the likeness of His own Mother. God is not an image of man, but man is of God; likewise, the Church is the image of Mary, not Mary of the Church.' (*La Mère de Dieu et la Mère des hommes*, 2ᵉ partie vol. II, chap. I).

The same mother who watched over the cradle of the Infant God, was present at the birth of the Church, for Pentecost is for ever linked with the mystery of Christmas.

Think of the grace that Our Lady's presence was to the infant Church. Fr. M. de la Taille in his famous work, *Mysterium fidei*, speaks of the influence of the most blessed Virgin on the holy sacrifices celebrated during her lifetime, and attributes to it in a special manner the wonderful growth of Christianity, and the abundance of miracles and of special graces that the Holy Ghost worked in the Church of her day.[46]

That presence of Our Lady meant grace also for St. John, whose especial teacher she was so much so that if St. John the Evangelist, speaks more divinely of God's mysteries than do his colleagues, it is, according to St. Ambrose, 'because he had near to Him the Sanctuary of Heaven's secrets.'[47] What grace indeed for all the evangelists, who were able directly or indirectly, to quench their thirst at such a spring, and pass on to us its living water.

And this union of Mary with the Church continues. Whenever today, in the name of the Church, we offer the Eucharistic sacrifice, which is identical with that of the Cross, we offer it in the name of Mary and in union with her, for Mary plays a large part in the very idea of the Church as its most distinguished member after Christ, Who is its Head.

If we have somewhat emphasized this connection between Mary and the Church, it is to show how deep-rooted is the Catholic and ecclesiological character of the Legion. Love of Mary, love of the Church: it is one and the same thing for the Legionary. He should not be afraid to go the whole length of his faith, and to see in the Church, 'Jesus Christ, communicated and outpoured.'

This will endow him with filial piety towards Him whom St.

Catherine of Sienna called *dolce Cristo in terra*, his Holiness the Pope. Every Legionary should keep in his heart the words of O'Connell, who wrote in his will, 'My body I leave to Ireland, my heart to Rome and my soul to Heaven.' Our hearts belong to Rome, because there the hearts of Christ and of Mary beat most strongly.

To love Mary is to love the Pope and receive his commands with respect, gratitude and joy. 'Lord, to whom shall we go?' asked the apostles, 'thou hast the words of eternal life.' Peter, living amongst us, is still the final refuge, the light which deceives not.

We should receive his Encyclicals, not to seek in them the sentences that please us, and confirm our personal opinions, but to enter fully into their thought, which is the breath of life, to accept completely and to live their message. We should spread around us knowledge of these instructions of peace, social reconciliation and spiritual and apostolic life.

Love of Mary is love of the bishop who, in his local Church, is the representative of Christ amongst us. 'He that heareth you heareth Me,' said Jesus. With that in mind we shall not stress his weakness nor his deficiencies, but shall see in him the shepherd of the sheep, the genuine teacher of religious truth.

Love of Mary is love of the priest whom we encounter daily, and who brings into the details of our ordinary lives the blessings of the Church. For him the Legion requires that respect and obedience which are his due, and 'yet more than this' (Manual). This demonstration of trust will be for the priest in his solitude, both stimulant and support. It will make of each Praesidium a hearth where all gather joyfully around their common father, and acquire new strength for the battles they fight together.

2. *Mary and the Church in the World today.*

The Legion of Mary means to be the Legion of the Church: it embraces her extension, cares and hopes. It is its ambition to be in our modern world 'that high enterprise for God' spoken of in the Manual, the advance guard facing the enemy.

The world we see appears to be submerged under a wave of materialism sweeping away all Christian life, and even all merely human life. In the name of a pseudo-gospel of godless brotherhood it would tear out man's soul and his whole reason for existence. Forbidden access to Heaven, he is chained to earth by promises of a future paradise here below. This ideal has its prophets and its slaves. Whether we will or no, the struggle is taking on gigantic proportions. The question is this: will the world see the triumph of Christ or of Antichrist? Everything else is child's play beside this battle with no quarter given. For no compromise is possible; sides must be taken for or against God, for or against the Church.

Two outlooks on life stand opposed. It is no time for half-measures, for hollow arguments or easy slogans: it is the time for heroic action, supreme witness. On a scale of world dimensions the future of civilization lies at stake before our eyes. What will govern this future? The armies of evil, drawing their ultimate inspiration from Satan, or the armies of God with St. Michael and his angels still today, invisibly at their head? Behind the agitation and intrigue of those in the forefront of the stage, a gigantic struggle is being waged: angels and devils pitted together, today more than ever before, for the perdition or salvation of humanity. This conflict far surpasses all our forecasts and estimates of strength. At the head of the infernal hordes 'who wander through the world for the ruins of souls' is Satan. Guiding the heavenly hosts—the heavenly legion—is Mary, Queen of Angels, whose chosen lieutenant is St. Michael. He who said 'No' to God is at grips with her who said 'Yes.' This is the real interpretation of the present age, the only philosophy of history which goes back to ultimate causes. The Legion of Mary—visible and tangible—is for its own part only an outer wing of the invisible army, marching under the generalship of the Queen of Heaven and earth.

That fact gives the true measure of the battle for God which is to be won.

For the Legion never despairs of final victory. 'A way exists,' it says, 'to bring back to the faith these millions of hardened apostates and of saving a multitude of others: one has just to apply the grand principle which, as formulated by the Curé d'Ars, rules the world. "The world belongs to him who loves it most and proves his love." Thousands of unfortunates, doubtless, will not listen to expositions of our faith, but they cannot fail to notice and be deeply touched by the heroic love for our neighbour which that faith inspires. Persuade them that the Church loves them best and they will soon turn their backs upon those who mislead. In spite of everything they will return to and even die for the Faith.'

He who loves the world with the heart of Mary knows that he loves with the strongest love: he holds in his hands limitless power, for no love for man can equal that of their Mother.

That is why the Legion looks realistically on the raging battle with neither illusion nor fear. It lives with the Church and feels every blow wherever in the world she suffers it. It delights in each report of victory and rejoices with the angels over every 'repentant sinner who returns to the fold.' It suffers from every wound, and exults whenever evil is forced to retire. It is as sensitive as a mother to the cry of the wounded, or the call for help of the soul in sin.

*
* *

In this immense struggle all the forces of God must unite for the salvation of humanity. That is why, no doubt, the Church is experiencing, at present, with renewed keenness, a longing for the return of our separated brethren to her unity. This problem dominates all others: now or never is the time to remember that Jesus Himself bound up Christian unity with belief in His mission *Ut sint unum*! 'That they all may be one, as Thou, Father, in Me, and I in Thee . . . that the world may believe that Thou hast sent Me.'

Frequently in history, attempts have been made to resolve this problem by learned and skilful discussions; often they have brought bitterness into the differences: they have never achieved lasting results.

Here again it seems that Mary's hour has come.

When children have left their home and no longer understand one another, does not the memory of their tenderly loved mother remain the strongest link between them and the best hope of seeing the family reconciled.

Mary is a mother like no other; she is the warmth of the home. She calls her children to press themselves against her heart. Close to her they will realize how much they are brothers, one of another.

Return to the unity of the Church through return to the common love of Mary. What a wonderful dream! Why should it be forbidden to believe that rivalry in active devotion towards Our Lady will one day reunite our separated brethren? It would be a task greatly after a mother's heart. Is that Utopian? Not at all, for Marian devotion, which is finding among Anglicans willing expression and is returning to certain Protestant groups, has remained vigorous and profound in the immense world of the Orient with Russia as its principal stronghold.

Not without reason, Pius XII spoke of this people who hid their ikons of Our Lady, but still venerated them lovingly.

Mary, the beloved of all, what hope there is in that!

Mary offers herself to us as the connecting link between Eastern and Western Christianity. She is a common blessing, a priceless treasure, passionately beloved. Let each then, open his soul to her that she may take possession of it. Mary will lead her children with a sure and gentle hand to the one fold where the whole truth is to be found, the fullness of life, Jesus Christ, Our Lord.

For its part, the Legion desires to hasten the time of union by offering to Mary souls ready for service, and responsive to her fashioning. Mary will deliver them to the Holy Ghost and He will make of these souls the docile instruments of His mighty plans, to accomplish His will, and work those wonders of grace which will renew the face of the earth, to the greater glory of God.

CHAPTER XI.

THE SIGN OF THE CROSS

IN THE NAME OF THE FATHER AND OF THE SON AND OF THE HOLY GHOST. AMEN.

1. *Suffering and the Apostolate.*

THE PROMISE is concluded by the sign of the Cross.

This is no meaningless gesture, or purely conventional rite. It is God's blessing coming down upon the Legionary and upon the pledge he has just made, enveloping him with invisible armour, for he knows that to take part in the apostolate is to enter into a mystery of Redemption, a mystery of death and of life. At every step he will find himself at grips with human suffering in numberless forms; he will encounter it in the souls that he will approach in the course of his visits and he must teach them, with tact and patience, the secrets of beneficial suffering. He will feel within himself, too, that souls cost dear, and sometimes he will emerge tired and bruised from this struggle against hell. The apostolate is not child's play, and God wants us to stake our very lives in this battle. The Legionary should look straight at the Cross which stands on Calvary and controls the salvation of men. If our Saviour paid for souls with His Blood, naturally the work of salvation undertaken by the Legionary also has its price: the disciple is not greater than his master. If he is not to be cast down by the first blow he must meditate deeply on the redemptive meaning of suffering. He must believe, for himself and for others, in the victorious love of God ever hidden in the depths of grief. If only he could truly believe that every suffering is a grace. 'Then,' says the Manual, 'the sense of suffering becomes the sense of Christ's close presence.' On the sole condition of ascribing all to God. It is not hard to believe that God loves us when all is going according to our wishes; but we need a well-seasoned faith if we are not to waver when the tempest breaks over our boat. Yet the love of God is more pressing and more enveloping than ever when we are in distress. We understand so ill the assaults of this love which baffles us. We fail to surrender ourselves to a tenderness which breaks us, the better to enable its waves to beat upon us. We doubt God because our faith is not strong enough to recognize Him beneath the frequently disconcerting disguises, under which He hides Himself. What unbelief lies at the heart of our faith!

We might humbly make our own this avowal and appeal of a chosen soul: 'My God, teach me to recognise your action in everything, in every creature that hurts me, in every happening which crosses me, as much as in every joy that delights me. Give me to understand in practice that if secondary causes are infinitely varied, there is but one first cause, and that first cause is you, Lord. The hand is the same, though the glove may be changed; it has its velvet glove, its horsehair glove, and its iron glove, according as its touch comforts or afflicts me. O God, my God, it is always your good tender hand which clasps mine, to tell me, "I love you." But however gentle the hand, when it grips with an iron glove, it is cold and hard, if not actually painful. . . . With a horsehair glove it is, at the least, trying. But we should like never to feel any but the velvet glove, but that one, Lord, you seem to use more sparingly than the others. . . . Do as you will, my Master, do not stand on ceremony with me: wear whichever glove you please, and squeeze my hand, as tightly as you like. Allow me only the filial privilege of removing the glove to kiss your hand.'

If the Legionary could understand in this way the nearness of God in all the suffering which he encounters, how much help he could bring to his brother, baffled by trials and plunged in darkness. He would console and strengthen him. Let him go to his brother in all gentleness, telling him that 'dawn begins at midnight,' that God is at work in his sore-tried soul, and that some day he will realize what wonders are taking place, unknown to him, in the depths of his heart. Let him quote the words of St. Louise-Marie, 'Leave God free to work; He loves you. He knows what He is about. He is experienced. He never strikes a blow that is not adroit and loving, never makes a false stroke, unless by your impatience you make His gesture useless. . . .' Or again, these bold words which the saint addressed to those whom he called 'the Friends of the Cross': 'Never receive any cross without kissing it with humility and thanksgiving, and when the good God has favoured you with some rather heavy ones give Him special thanks and cause others to thank Him too.' It is good to measure our faith by that of the saints, so as to see our wretchedness as 'believing unbelievers': and our inconsistency as Christians, so little aware of baptism that we remain more than semi-pagan. If only we could discover, through the saints, a full-blooded Christianity, the only kind that has the words of eternal life. We shall not, at once, speak to our suffering brother words too heavy with spiritual meaning, but keep them in our hearts, so that their diffused light and hidden warmth may penetrate the encouraging words of comfort we use, in the hope that he—and we too—may one day be able to bear them.

What a change there would be if we only dared to believe that suffering in every form is the great highway to intimacy with God, the way to decisive meetings with His love. Of course it is normal for nature to recoil at suffering and Jesus Himself, so greatly did He feel Himself a man like us, prayed in the Garden of Olives, that the chalice might pass from Him. Despite the blessed certainty that His agony was to save the world, our Saviour's first reaction was distress and disgust. *Coepit taedere et moestus esse.* Blessed be those sacred words which help us not to blush at our cowardice and terrors. Blessed be Christ who simultaneously trembled before death and went forward to it with calm steps to show us by the same token that He is one of us, and that we must follow in His footsteps.

To help us to overcome this instinctive recoil, we should realize that the cross presented to us, is not just any suffering, dictated by caprice or blind fate, but a gift from God, especially chosen from very many and fitted to our stature. 'Let this man carry courageously his cross on his shoulders, and not that of another,' St. Louis-Marie puts into the mouth of God, 'his cross that in My wisdom I have made especially for him in number, size and weight; his cross which with My own hand I have shaped with exceeding accuracy in its four dimensions of thickness, breadth, length and depth; his cross that I have cut out for him from part of that which I carried to Calvary. . . .'

If we grasped better, that nothing is left to chance in the world, that the love of God is ever on the watch, that He knows infinitely better than we do what is good for us, we should be less afraid of leaving ourselves in His hands and of receiving such precious gifts from them. It is enough to believe that 'to them that love God, all things work together unto good,' and that the good He wills is not just any good, but the best possible since it is willed by God and given in a God-like manner, that is, charged to the highest degree with His victorious grace.

The Legionary should believe this for himself; he should believe it also on behalf of others and impart to them as good tidings, this Christian outlook on suffering. To the wounded in life's battles, he should act as an interpreter of God.

Besides, the apostolate will be often, of its very nature, a cross to carry. The conquest of souls demands a heavy price. The greatest trial of the apostolate is not, as might be thought, the hostility of sinners, but the lack of support on the part of those who should help in the work. The Manual devotes a whole paragraph, pregnant with human experience, to this rock on which we may come to grief. Under the title: 'The sign of the Cross is the sign of hope,' it has these lines:

'It must always be remembered that the work of the Lord will bear the Lord's own mark, the mark of the Cross. Without that imprint, the supernatural character of a work may be doubted; true results will not be forthcoming. Janet Erskine Stuart states this principle in another way. "If you look," she says, "at sacred history, Church history and even at your own experience, which each year must add to, you will see that God's work is never done in ideal conditions, never as we should have imagined or chosen." That is to say—amazing thought—that the very circumstances which to the limited human vision, seems to prevent those conditions from being ideal, and to spoil the prospects of the work, is not an obstacle to success, but the requisite for success ... not a deadweight on effort, but fuel which feeds that effort and aids it to achieve its purpose. For it is ever God's pleasure to show His power by extracting success from unpromising conditions and by accomplishing His greatest projects with inadequate instruments.'

Everyone knows the disappointing experience of the obstacles set in the way of the apostolate by good people. Not, certainly through evil intent, but due to the mere action of human narrowness, through the clashing of points of view, when wider vision would bring complementary truths into harmony. Few can understand that 'nightfall does not contradict dawn, and that the Autumn of the year is not a denial of Spring.' We should face this cross heavier though it is, perhaps, than many another. In this way God purifies His instruments, refines, detaches them from themselves, and gives to them a more acute and discerning perception of His unique glory. One day we shall see how all this interplay of light and shade was an integral part of the Redemption of souls.

And then we shall give thanks to God for every stone met on the road, every desert we had to cross, every well, which should have quenched our thirst, whose waters proved sadly bitter. All this God has willed, or at least allowed; all this He has weighed up and lovingly taken into account. *Posuisti lacrymas in conspectu tuo Domine*. The Lord has looked on our tears as pearls of great price shining eternally before His Face. It is good to know this, not that we may look complacently into ourselves, but that we may go joyfully forward, lifting up our heads bravely, beneath the storm, and recognize the signs of 'approaching Redemption.' *Levate capita vestra quia appropinquat redemptio vestra*. This conviction helps the Legionary to penetrate more deeply the meaning of the saying which the Manual has given to him as a direction: 'Success is a joy: a check is but delayed success.' This comprehension of the cross will enable him to act up to the ideal of constancy that the Legion desires to inspire, and which it describes in these words:

'It does not require from its members wealth or influence, but faith unwavering: not famous deeds but only unrelaxed effort: not genius but unquenchable love: not giant strength but steady discipline.

A Legionary service must be one of holding on, of absolute and obstinate refusal to lose heart. A rock in the crisis: but constant at all times.

Hoping for success, humble in success: but independent of it. Fighting failure; undismayed by it: fighting on and wearing it down.

Unmindful of self: all the time standing by the Cross of others, and standing there till the work is consummated.'

2. *The Compassion of Mary.*

Apostolate means Redemption. The artisan of Redemption is Jesus Christ, without Whom there is no salvation. But at the foot of the Cross on Calvary stood a woman who in her heart offered the unique sacrifice in our name. Mary, Co-redemptress, united her compassion with the Passion of her Son. Marian theology makes increasingly clear the importance of this presence and the meaning of this direct co-operation. Here, more than ever, we must avoid all ambiguity. We repeat: Our Lord Jesus Christ alone is Redeemer of the world, in the true and proper sense of the word. No one shares this glory with Him, and Mary, though in a manner different from ours, had her own need of this unique Redemption. The absolute sufficiency of Our Lord's Blood does not, however, prevent the Church from recognizing that in a secondary and derivative sense, by participation, all the elect co-operate in the Redemption of the world. And amongst the elect it is very evident that Mary holds a supereminent position. But her role is not limited to this subsequent co-operation. There are her inexpressible sorrows, and still more her full consent, her voluntary adherence to the sacrifice of her Son; this endows her co-operation in the Redemption of the world with a unique character. Doubtless, the 'fiat' of the Annunciation included already the 'fiat' of Calvary, since the Child who was to be born of her was to be the price of atonement, but at the foot of the Cross in her heart, Mary completed what God did not finally require of Abraham: the immolation of her only Son. Thereby Mary, from her own place, of course, entered deeper than any other human creature into the mystery of the Redemptive sacrifice. Thereby she ratifies, in the name of all, the unique oblation. The Legionary will understand that the apostolate which he desires to accomplish in union with her should in its turn be rooted in this compassion of the most blessed Virgin. Mary will reveal to him new grounds for esteeming a soul, redeemed at so great a price, and the immense evil of sin, atoned for by so great a holocaust. She will teach him to kiss those sacred wounds with infinite gratitude and to tell his crucified Lord: *vulnera tua merita mea*, 'Thy wounds are my merits.' She will give him a mother's attitude to the sinner who for his part also commits deicide, but knows not what he does. The Legionary, looking at the sins of the world through Mary's eyes, will relive in his heart the scene of the Crucifixion of God. 'For God,' as it has so well been put, 'lives not only in Heaven: He lives also in souls and no life is frailer or more threatened than that. Nothing in the world is so easily killed or so easily doomed as that life of God in man; the smallest blow of self-interest or passion, the slightest pressure of conformism is enough to kill it; here Supreme Reality has made Himself timorous, as easily swept away as a dream, and that is why the love of saints is so tender, so greatly imbued with pity, so trembling with simultaneous hope and fear. Every day they fight for the very life of their God.'(48)

The Legionary will feel, too, the need of uniting his compassion with the Sacrifice which compelled pardon. And he will be glad to be able to bring to the Master that measure of suffering which his duty imposes, and those additional mortifications inevitably imposed by the apostolate. He will say 'yes' to God in place of those who refuse His grace: he will be jealously faithful in place of those who sin against the light: he will stand beside Mary at the foot of the Cross in place of those who fled, betrayed and denied; in union with Mary he will gather into his heart all human suffering which is unsanctified by acceptance and cannot, therefore, achieve its purpose as God's sacrament; in place of the rebellious he will utter the 'fiat' of that surrender which transfigures. Through his compassion he will turn to a successful result all that suffering scattered so widely over the face of the earth, directing its flow to a happy issue, as a powerful river in its course gathers, despite themselves, all rebellious waters to empty them finally into the sea. He will obtain this outlet by the petition in the Lord's prayer: 'Thy Kingdom come, Thy will be done on earth as it is in Heaven.' It is a marvellous role, a splendid mission, to make God's glory stand out clearly in this way from beneath the sorrows of men, where it lies hidden, and to throw their distress into the arms of His mercy. He will renew this gesture in union with Mary, especially when he unites himself with the culminating prayer of the Canon of the Mass; *Per ipsum et cum ipso et in ipso est tibi Deo Patri omnipotenti in unitate Spiritus Sancti omnis honor, et gloria, per omnia saecula saeculorum. Amen.* Consider what this prayer means on the lips of the most Blessed Virgin, this doxology, which sums up her whole attitude of soul at the foot of the Cross.

Better than anyone, Mary understood the mystery of glory which was accomplished before her eyes on that Good Friday. In silence she adored 'God who was Christ reconciling the world to Himself.' Her soul enjoyed the peace of an invincible certainty: light had triumphed over darkness; love over hatred; good over evil. Here already was the first comfort of the dawn—the Easter dawn.

3. *The Sign of the Cross.*

All this the sign of the Cross recalls to our minds. The veneration with which the Church surrounds it should not, therefore, cause surprise. Not one action of importance in life is accomplished without her making this sign of the Redemption: over the child she baptizes or confirms, over the Host she proffers, the sinner she absolves, the love she sanctifies, the priest she consecrates and the dying man she comforts. She makes it, too, over the bread, the water, salt or oil that we shall eat, our growing crops and workshops. She uses this sign on numberless occasions, opposing the devil with tranquil assurance: *In hoc signo vinces,* 'In this sign thou shalt conquer.'

So it is fitting to set out on our apostolic tasks strengthened and fortified by this sign of God. We must keep the sense of this sacred gesture which is at the same time the most glorious profession of faith.

4. *Profession of Faith in the Trinity.*

For the sign of the Cross is simultaneously expression of belief in the Trinity:

In the name of the Father and of the Son and of the Holy Ghost.
With this all things are begun, with this they are all brought

to completion. The love of God, we said, is the origin of all things, and it should be added, provides the key to the mystery of creation. The vision of the holy Trinity should dominate and animate the whole of Christian life, and that vision is the goal of all apostolic work.

In Nomine Patris: In the name of the Father.

Why set out to win souls? So that men may live as sons of God. Any other life falls short of their destiny. What are the 'good tidings' that we carry to our brethren? That there is in Heaven a God who is their Father, and that He has put them in the world solely to make them sharers of His life and its benefits. Nothing is more urgent than to repeat to men the end to which their creation tends, the thought of God for each individual. They need this message as they need air. They need it for mutual love, for it is in this Fatherhood of God that brotherly love has its roots.

In the name of the Father.

Do not say: 'I do not know that man,' but in him I recognize a son of my Father; I feel united to him by bonds stronger than blood; a common calling destines us both for the same home. I will go to that man; I *do* know him.

In the name of the Father.

The Legionary will go thus to all 'prodigals' who have left their father's home and dissipated their share of the inheritance. He will tell them that their own place is set for them at the family table, and that the Father climbs every evening to the top of the hill to watch for their return. The eldest brother in the parable knew only the personal satisfaction of duty done. The Legionary knows better; he goes out into the street to seek the wanderer; he brings to them the persistent love of the Father and His untiring forgiveness, nor does he desist until he leads home the penitent and with his own hand kills the fatted calf.

In the name of the Father.

We should be more keenly aware of our position as 'naturalized citizens' of heaven if we, too, should 'be about our Father's business.'

After all, what is really important? One thing alone: that the Father should be able to communicate Himself to His children, that His glory be manifested and His will be done.

In Nomine Filii: in the name of the Son.

The Church knows the strength of this formidable name which vanquished Satan and wrested his empire from him; and she is fond of making it resound in her exorcisms. Listen to this:

'We exorcise thee, unclean spirit whoever thou art, power of Satan, in the Name and in the power of Jesus Christ our Lord, be thou torn from and driven out from God's church, from the souls created to the likeness of God and redeemed by the precious Blood of the Lamb of God. . . .

'Be humbled beneath the mighty hand of God: tremble and fly away at the invocation we make of the holy and terrible name of Jesus, which hell fears, to which the Virtues of Heaven and Dominations submit, whom Cherubim and Seraphim ceaselessly praise together saying Holy, Holy, Holy is the Lord, God of Hosts.'

With the Church we should have the courage to believe in the almighty power of this triumphant name.

In the name of the Son.

He conquered the sin of man, and keeps in reserve for souls to come the superabundant price of His victory. We should dare to believe that if we fight against evil, armed with this name, we have with us all the power of God.

In the name of the Son.

He has overcome the world, and for this reason, expects us to advance confidently to its conquest. We should dare to believe that through us He will do still greater things than He did Himself. Such is His promise.

In the name of the Son.

He vanquished death when He emerged alive from the tomb on

Easter morning; by His death was death killed. We should dare to believe that no tombstone is too heavy to lift by the invocation of that name; that no tomb is too strongly sealed for Him to push aside, and that He laughs at the guards whom hate and fear have posted to give the lie to His words.

In the name of the Son.

He overcame the anger of God and won from Him pardon for all the guilty, for all prodigals, for all Magdalens. We should dare to believe that we are not alone when we fight to save the hardened sinner from himself and the anger of God, and that, in and through us, Christ desires to be for that man the resurrection and the life.

In the name of the Son.

He gave orders to preach the Gospel to every creature and promised to be with us until the end of time. We should dare to believe that God gives grace in proportion to His orders, and even far beyond our boldest hopes.

In Nomine Spiritus Sancti: in the name of the Holy Ghost.

Have we thought how wonderful is this mission entrusted to us by God: to go to men in the strength and virtue of His love for them, *in Spiritu Sancto*? Not to love them with our feeble love, but to love them with His infinite heart, that is, with a love which knows no barriers, which nothing can rebuff; a love which knows how to wait, to make ceaseless beginnings, tirelessly, without taking offence, or needing due thanks; a love which sinks as low as the lowest human misery, unafraid of being sullied by the most repugnant contact; a love which can be as violent as a gale, tears out evil by the very roots, and lances the abscess, yet can be as gentle as a breeze, can cure the wounded by sheer patience, and will not quench the smoking flax. A love which returns to the attack unwearying as the mighty waves: they break themselves against the cliffs, but nevertheless, beat ceaselessly in rhythm with wind and tide, against the rocks which finally crumble or split. A love too, which can listen with tact greater than a mother's, to the confidences which lead to confession and conversion, which understands the unique character of each soul, and helps it to hear its individual call from God.

In the name of the Holy Ghost.

What an invitation to daring. Thanks to the Holy Ghost we have the right to go forth to men with the courage born of conviction that Another is at work through us, lending us His light and His power. We have the right to believe that God's Holy Spirit will be the inspiration of our thoughts and the breath of our mouths.

In the name of the Holy Ghost.

It is as though we ourselves emerged from the Cenacle on the morning of Pentecost to proclaim to the crowds that life has a new meaning since Christ came forth alive from the tomb, and that God is reconciled with man.

In the name of the Holy Ghost.

We have to tear men from themselves, teach them of beatitude unsuspected, upset their scale of values, and lead them to receive the grace of holiness and life which surpass all understanding.

We have to renew the face of the earth in the likeness of the Son, to the glory of the Father. And it is the Spirit who requires us to co-operate, with all our hearts in this unique work that He pursues untiring, down the centuries, for our joy and His glory.

NOTES

[1] An account of its origin has been given by Frank Duff, founder of the Legion, in the review *Maria Legionis* (Dublin), 1937-42. This account, unfortunately incomplete, has pages which are unique in the annals of Contemporary Catholic apostolate.

The official explanation of the nature and function of the Legion is given in its Handbook, published in English and translated into French, Dutch, German, Spanish, Italian, Tamil, Malayan, Sinhalese and Chinese. Russian, Polish and Japanese translations exist but have not yet been published.

The prayers proper to the Legion (Tessera) are recited in some seventy different languages.

[2] Francis Thompson; *The Hound of Heaven*.

[3] The Encyclical *Mystici Corporis* recalls the undisputed principle in these words: 'In these matters all things are to be held common to the Blessed Trinity, so far as the same relate to God as the supreme efficient cause.' This is valid for every *created* effect, and is thus applicable to created, sanctifying grace which accompanies the indwelling of the Holy Spirit. But this principle is not applicable to the Holy Spirit Himself, in as much as He is a presence and an *uncreated* gift.

[4] Cf. Mgr. Lebon, préface to the French translation of the *Letters to Serapion*, *Lettres à Sérapion* in the *Sources chrétiennes* series, n. 15, Paris, 1947, pp. 52-77.

[5] Come thou Father of the poor,
What is soiled make thou pure,
What is wounded Thou canst cure,
Water what is hard and dry,
What is rigid gently bend,
What is frozen warmly tend,
Strengthen what goes erringly.

[6] It must be stated, once and for all, that in quoting Mariological text from Holy Scripture, we do not mean to interpret them in isolation from the context. We consider them always in relation to the whole of divine thought which places them in proper perspective, and to living tradition as it is experienced and prayed by the Church which perpetuates them. The Scriptures are sparing in references to Our Lady, but there must be no mistaken ideas about this silence. When it is said of a creature that she is the Mother of Jesus and that Jesus is God, there is not one single word that can be added to her praise and glory; an eternity cannot exhaust the disclosure of her greatness. It is from this point of view that we must understand the method here employed. Modern 'Mariology' is based on the Scriptures as they are interpreted by the Church in her

liturgy, and by the Fathers in their commentaries on the Bible. The Church takes the Bible as a *whole*. She takes the converging themes of the Divine Word; she makes known their mysterious connection which lies at the heart of a unique mystery. For example the theme of the Betrothal is among them; that of the Temple and of the Messianic feast are others. There is no question, then, of taking isolated texts from the Bible where it speaks of Mary; they must be taken together. In this sense the exegesis which we use here is not 'literal.' It is in accordance, however, with the sense 'willed by God' because the whole of tradition makes it evident that it is in this converging light that the Church sees things and that this view is the same as God's. The Church, the bride of Jesus, alone can hear the Voice of her Bridegroom and fathom the secrets of God, *arcana Dei*. (Cf. Charlier, *La lecture chrétienne de la Bible*, Maredsous, 1950).

7 'In uno igitur eodemque alvo castissimae Matris et carnem Christus assumpsit et spirituale simul corpus adjunxit, ex iis nempe coagmentatum qui credituri erant in eum. Ita ut Salvatorem habens Maria in utero, illos etiam dici queat gessise omnes, quorum vitam continebat vita Salvatoris. Universo ergo, quotquot cum Christo jungimur, quique, ut ait Apostolus, membra sumus corporis ejus, de carne ejus et de ossibus ejus (*Ephes.*, V, 30), de Mariae utero egressi sumus, tanquam corporis instar cohaerentes cum capite. Unde spiritali quidem ratione ac mystica, et Mariae filii nos dicimur, et ipsa nostrum omnium mater est. Mater quidem spiritu ... sed plane mater membrorum Christi, quod nos sumus.' The same teaching is to be found in the encyclical *Mystici Corporis* of Pius XII, where, summarizing the teaching of Pius X, he speaks of Mary as 'omnium membrorum Christi sanctissima Genitrix.'

8 Cf. M. V. Bernadot, O.P., *Our Lady in Our Life* (Mercier Press), or again, P. R. Bernard, O.P., *Le Mystère de Marie* (Desclée).

9 Cf. E. Tobac article on *Grâce* in the *Dictionnaire apologétique de la Foi Catholique*, II, 335; see also, on the same lines, L. Malevez, *Quelques enseignements de l'encyclique 'Mystici Corporis Christi,'* in the *Nouvelle Revue Théologique*, September-October, 1945.

10 E. Neubert, *Marie dans le dogme*, Paris, Spes, 2nd ed., p. 236.

11 Tradition regards Mary as the bride of Christ because it is the Son of God who is united to Mary by taking flesh in her womb. This is a classical theme. Certain painters have even depicted it by showing the Infant Jesus slipping a wedding ring on to His Mother's finger. This ancient and venerable tradition does not prevent Mary being called the bride of the Holy Spirit. For centuries the Church has used this title which she sanctions and of which the first traces are to be found from the beginning of the twelfth century, in the writings of Nicholas of Clairvaux, Amadeus of Lausanne and Conrad of Saxony. The reality of the mysteries of God is so rich that the aspects which we distinguish are complementary rather than exclusive. In these pages we shall put particular emphasis on the

relationship between Mary and the Holy Spirit; but it should not be forgotten for a moment that their very union is the cause of that other alliance which makes Mary the bride of the Incarnate Word. All the same it is proper to bear in mind that if the expression 'Bride of the Holy Ghost' can be applied to Mary, the Holy Ghost does not thereby become the father of Jesus any more than does the Word, if we make use of the expression *Sponsa Verbi* (Bride of the Word). The Holy Ghost does not draw the humanity of Christ from His own substance; the operation of the Holy Spirit results in the formation of Christ in His humanity. He does not intervene as a constituent element of it. The two expressions 'Bride of the Word' or 'Bride of the Holy Spirit' should, then, be used with tact and prudence. In these pages of commentary on the Promise, which is addressed to the Holy Spirit, it is natural that the expression *sponsa Spiritus*, should be used to express a certain relationship between Mary and the Holy Spirit. All the same we make no claim to confining relationship between them within this one formula.

[12] Dante, *Paradiso*, XXXII, 85.

[13] *Treatise on True Devotion to the Blessed Virgin*, n. 164. (References are to the translation, published by the Montfort Fathers, Montfort College, Romsey, Hants., 1942—the Centenary edition).

[14] This character of 'openness'—*ad alium*—a tending towards others—of true personality would deserve a special and more extended study which would be the exact opposite of the philosophy of despair proclaiming that 'Hell is other people;' it would show that 'Heaven is other people.' We mention here for the guidance of readers: R. C. Moberly, *Atonement and Personality*, 1901. Blondel, *L'Action*. Zundel, *Notre-Dame de la Sagesse*. De Régnon, *Etudes de Théologie Positive sur la Sainte Trinité*. Henry, *On some implications of the 'Ex Patre Filioque tanquam ab uno principio,'* an article in the special number 'Concerning the Holy Spirit' of *The Eastern Churches Quarterly*, 1928, p. 22. Nedoncelle, *Essai sur la communication des consciences*, Paris, Aubier.

[15] *Ad diem illum*, 1904.

[16] We consider that no harmonious and reliable account of the mysterious interplay between grace and free will can be given unless Mary and the Holy Spirit are seen in their proper place. As an Anglican writer has noted with remarkable exactitude: 'Thanks to Mary's co-operation by her *fiat* the Eternal Word was made flesh. That is why she is the cause of our joy. The part played by the human response to the call of God cannot be clearly grasped and understood except in the light of a balanced Mariology.' *Nouvelle Revue Théologique*, 1949, p. 270.

[17] 'Exspectabatur consensus Virginis loco totius humanae naturae.' S. Th. III, q. 30, art. I, sed c. et concl.

'Consensus Beatae Virginis qui per annuntiationem requirebatur actus singularis personae erat in multitudinis salutem redundans, imo totius humani generis.' III *Sent.*, dist. 3, q. 3, art. 2, sol. 2-3.

18 Father Louis Bouyer of the Oratory, recently wrote these lines:
'Mary, at the beginning of the Church, represents as concentrated in one person, the same perfection that will be displayed finally in the multitude of believers gathered together in Unity. She is thus the symbol and pledge of Catholic unity.' *Irénikon*, Vol. II, 1949, p.150.
19 *Treatise on True Devotion to the Blessed Virgin*, n. 5.
20 *The Secret of Mary*, n. 9.
21 *Treatise on True Devotion to the Blessed Virgin*, n. 36.
22 Cf. his Mariology, especially the chapter devoted to Mary's personal character and that which examines her mediation.
23 *Oratio ad Deiparam* (Ed. Assemani, graec. lat., vol. III, p. 528). 'First after the Trinity, best comforter after the Paraclete.'
24 It should not be forgotten, however, that according to tradition, the Holy Spirit, though essentially the 'Revealing Person,' does not reveal Himself *directly*. There is, as it were, a mystery of the humility and self-effacement of the Holy Spirit. The Holy Spirit is essentially a bond of union and love. He is turned especially in the direction of Christ's gift to men. In the same way that He formed Christ in Mary, so He forms Him in the Church. It is in the Holy Spirit that we become transformed, that gradually we put on Christ. Devotion to the most blessed Virgin quite naturally turns the Christian towards greater devotion to the Holy Spirit. But this devotion of its very nature is Christocentric.
25 3rd Sermon for the feast of the Immaculate Conception.
26 *La Théologie du Corps mystique*, vol. I, p. 215. et seq.
27 For a better understanding of the closeness of our union with Mary, we consider it of use to quote here, a fine passage by Jean Guitton:
'Mary is not absent from this world. None of the saints, no soul, none of our departed is at a distance from this world. And we are wrong in imagining the other world as something distant. It is a weakness to be unable to imagine the transcendent, save by the device of distance and to place in a sort of stratosphere that which is more intimate than ourselves.

'If we cannot imagine the "Other World," I suggest that we see it as a sphere which envelops this world, or rather as a series of spheres lucid and concentric, in the same way that Ptolemy represented the concentric heavens. The most enveloping sphere would be the eternal Christ in whom we are and move and have our being. The more immediate sphere (that which touches us most closely and sensibly) would be the departed: a mother, wife, child or friend—in whom we live and move and have our being.

'Between this small sphere, which is personal to us, and that greater sphere, I can conceive intermediary ones. Such is the Marian sphere . . . . I do not view that which lies beyond Mary as something distant but as enveloping. And the spiritual problem which occurs in connection with her seems to me to be accurately defined by the words of Nicodemus:

it is a case, going back over and redeeming time, (as in the myth of the Platonic dialogue *Politics*), of becoming a child again, of re-entering this enfolding womb as if one went back again "aged in years to the mothers' womb."

'From this point of view the life of the spirit is the exact contrary to the life of the body. In the life of the spirit the farther the body retreats from the mother's womb, the more it grows and becomes strong; living means leaving this first environment in order to have a separate existence. But in this spiritual life, after the Marian pattern, a powerful though gentle influence, draws us away from the exterior and in some sort "involutes" us so as to incorporate us with Christ and the Holy Spirit into whom we return: this is effected by the agency of maternal likeness which is the Marian influence and sphere.'

Jean Guitton, *La Vierge Marie*, Aubier, series 'Les Religions,' pp. 207-8.

[28] This difference is brought out particularly clearly by St. Louis-Marie de Montfort in his *Treatise on True Devotion to the Blessed Virgin*, chapter VIII. See also: *La Doctrine Mariale de M. Chaminade*, by E. Neubert, Paris, Editions du Cerf, series 'Les Cahiers de la Vierge.'

[29] On the close union between Mary and the apostolate, there is an interesting chapter in *Marie dans le Dogme* by E. Neubert, entitled 'La Mission apostolique de Marie.'

[30] Canon Guynot, *Notre Dame de la Légion*, n. 1, p. 5: 'La charité légionnaire.'

[31] English original.

[32] Id.

[33] Id.

[34] See the article quoted, *Irénikon*, 1949, p. 516.

[35] *Summa Theologica*, III, q. 73, a. 5, ad 2.

[36] The treatment of the subject as it is here given, should be understood by taking into account the bond uniting Mary and the Church.

Prayer with the Church, union with the prayer of the Church, participation in the sacrifice of the Mass as the sacrifice of the Church, is all effected profoundly in union with Mary.

On the relationship between Mary and the Church, the reader will find interesting material in Hugo Rahner, S.J.: *Marie und die Kirche*, Innsbruck, 1951. See also Otto Semmelroth, S.J.: *Urbild der Kirche. Organischer Aufbau des Mariengeheimnisses*, Wurzburg, 1950.

[37] *Semaine Religieuse d'Angers*, September 29, 1939.

[38] Our Eastern brethren express their intense devotion to Mary in other forms: the Acathist hymn is a beautiful example of this. But they have no fear of repetitions of the same prayer for like us they know that the human heart is never surfeited with certain joys. Their particular preference is to repeat the Holy Name of Jesus. This Sacred Name is found by us, too, enshrined in the Ave Maria, like a pearl in its setting. Though customs differ, the objects of veneration remain the same. For it is very true that truth, in spite of variations of psychological

approach, remains indivisible and that the way of devotion to Our Lady must be that which leads us to Jesus.

39 M. Zundel, *Le Poéme de la Sainte Liturgie*, Paris, p. 375. Also English translation: *The Splendour of the Liturgy*, London, 1939.

40 'In utero situs matris a mensura perfectae coepit aetatis plenitudinis Christi.' St. Ambrose, *Comment. in Luc.*, II, 30.

'Non enim sola familiaritatis est causa quod diu mansit, sed etiam tanti vatis profectus. . . . Si primo ingressu tantus processus exstitit . . . quantum putamus usu tanti temporis sanctae Mariae addidisse praesentiam.' *Ibid.*, II, 29.

41 The greatness of St. Joseph, brought out very clearly by Leo XIII's Encyclical *Quam pluries*, (August 15, 1889), has been excellently summarized by Fr. M. Philipon, O.P., in these words: 'The transcendence of the sanctity of St. Joseph over the universality of angels and saints derives from his threefold mission, the highest after divine Maternity:

1. His role as head of the holy Family and by extension, his patronage over the Church of Christ.

2. His title as spouse of the Mother of God.

3. Lastly and above all, his paternal office over the Incarnate Word, the supreme source of his supereminent greatness: "ut Unigenitum tuum . . . paterna vice custodiret" (Preface).' *Le vrai visage de Notre-Dame*, p. 68, Paris, Desclée, De Brouwer, 1949.

42 J. Daniélou, *Le Mystère de l'Avent*, Paris, pp. 92-3. (English Translation: *Advent*, Sheed & Ward).

43 'Jesus Christ,' wrote Nicole, 'associates our Lady with His plan of forming a precursor by filling the soul of St. John the Baptist with grace. He desired that it should take place through her ministry. He gave her a part in the spiritual birth of St. John, even as she had taken part in the very mystery of the Incarnation. And as St. John represented the Church and all the elect, since it was said of him that he had been sent by God, that all might believe in him, (*John* 1, 7), Jesus Christ has shown us thereby, that Our Lady co-operates by her charity in the spiritual birth of the elect, and that when Jesus Christ visits them by His grace, she visits them by her charity by obtaining this grace for them through her intercession. Thus she is really our mother and we ought always to look on her as being as united to Jesus Christ in the words of grace He effects in us, as she was in that visit that she paid to Elizabeth and St. John.' Nicole, *Continuat. des Essais de Morale*, Pensees morales sur les mystères de Jésus-Christ, la Visitation, par. 2 and 3, *Oeuvres*, vol. XIII, pp. 331-2, Paris, 1741.

44 Bossuet wishing to depict the spiritual motherhood of the Church, puts it in this way: 'She is the mother of every individual who makes up the body of Christianity: she gives them birth for Jesus Christ, not as other mothers do by bringing them forth from her womb, but by drawing them from the outside to receive them into her womb by incorporating them with herself, and in her with the Holy Spirit, who gives them life,

and in the Holy Spirit with the Son, who gave us that Spirit by His breath, and by the Son with the Father, who sent Him so that our association might be in God and with God, Father, Son, and Holy Spirit.'

[45] Based on E. Druwé, S.J., *Position et structure du traité marial*, in the *Bulletin de la soc. franc. d'études mariales*, Paris, 1936, pp. 12-3.

[46] L.c. *Elucidatio XXVI*, p. 331, Paris, Beauchesne, 1924.

[47] Cf. St. Amrose, Institut, virg., c, 7, n. 5, *P.L. XVI*, 319. quoted in Terrien, *La Mère de Dieu et des hommes*, 2nd part vol. II, Paris, 2nd ed., p. 31.

[48] G. Thibon, *Ce que Dieu a uni*, Paris, H. Lardanchet, 1947, p. 194. (English translation, *What God has joined together*, Hollis and Carter, London, 1952).

Date Due

APR 29 '59			
JAN 5 '60			
APR 11 '60			
29 '60			
AUG 14 '59			
JA 21 '65			
FE 23 '65			
MR 21 '65			
NO 23 '66			

PRINTED IN U. S. A.

MARYGROVE COLLEGE LIBRARY
Theology of the apostolate of th
267.11 Su2t

3 1927 00113441 7

267.11
Su2t